The die is cast . . .

The evening before the abduction of Natascha Kampusch, Wolfgang Priklopil set about preparing. He checked that everything was ready in the special room. He laid out underpants and towels, arranged the children's books that he had bought in shops far, far from his neighborhood. And he programmed the security and ventilation systems one more time, ensuring that the compressed air pump that would keep his trophy alive was working, along with the plethora of intruder alarms and video cameras vital to keep his secret safe.

Shortly after 6 a.m. on Monday, March 2, as radio newscasters were informing him that it was the birthday of *perestroika* architect Mikhail Gorbachev, that the last will of the late Princess Diana had been published, and, closer to home, that a walker had discovered a 5-kilo anti-tank shell from the Second World War in a Viennese suburb, Priklopil drank his coffee, set the numerous alarms on his house, and went out into the wet, dark morning. He started his white Mercedes van and drove off for the rendezvous with the little girl who, on this day, would cross over the line from his special dream to his special possession.

Nothing could stop him now; nothing could save Natascha now.

ATTENTION: ORGANIZATIONS AND CORPORATIONS
Most Harper paperbacks are available at special quantity discounts
for bulk purchases for sales promotions, premiums, or fund raising.
For information, please call or write:

**Special Markets Department, HarperCollins Publishers,
10 East 53rd Street, New York, New York 10022-5299.
Telephone: (212) 207-7528.   Fax: (212) 207-7222.**

GIRL
IN THE
CELLAR

THE NATASCHA KAMPUSCH STORY

ALLAN HALL AND MICHAEL LEIDIG

HARPER

An Imprint of HarperCollinsPublishers

This book was originally published in Great Britain in 2006 by Hodder & Stoughton, a division of Hodder Headline, and in hardcover January 2007 by Harper.

Photographic acknowledgments (Insert pages 1-16): © ABC, Vienna: 16 bottom. © AP/Empics/Helmut Stamberg: 14 top. © Katarina Angerer/EuroPics(CEN): 11. Courtesy Bundeskriminalamt, Vienna: 2 bottom right, 5 top, 6 bottom, 9 bottom, 10 top, 12 top, 13 top. © EuroPics(CEN): 2. © EuroPics (CEN)/Grainger Laffan: 3 top, 4, 5 bottom, 6 top, 7 top, 9 top, 15. © EuroPics(CEN)/Michael Leidig: 16 top left. © First Look: 3 bottom. © Franz Gruber: 16 top right. © Junior Foto, Vienna: 1. © Österreich: 14 centre left. © Reuters: 8, 10 bottom, 12 bottom, 13 bottom. © Rex Features: 7 bottom (Sipa Press), 14 bottom (photo Karl Schoendorfer).

HARPER

An Imprint of HarperCollins*Publishers*
10 East 53rd Street
New York, New York 10022-5299

Copyright © 2007 by Allan Hall and Michael Leidig
ISBN 978-0-06-194529-8

All rights reserved. No part of this book may be used or reproduced in any manner whatsoever without written permission, except in the case of brief quotations embodied in critical articles and reviews. For information address Harper paperbacks, an Imprint of HarperCollins Publishers.

First Harper paperback printing: March 2010
First Harper hardcover printing: January 2007

HarperCollins® and Harper® are registered trademarks of Harper-Collins Publishers.

Printed in the United States of America

Visit Harper paperbacks on the World Wide Web at www.harpercollins.com

10 9 8 7 6 5 4 3 2

If you purchased this book without a cover, you should be aware that this book is stolen property. It was reported as "unsold and destroyed" to the publisher, and neither the author nor the publisher has received any payment for this "stripped book."

Dedication

This work was produced with the help of journalists Jakob Weichenberger, Katharina Oke, Jessica Spiegel, Paul Eidenberger, Jörg Michner, and many others.

This book is dedicated to all the missing children who have not been found and their families.

To my mother, Pamela and Oscar
Allan Hall

Contents

Foreword

Strasshof an der Nordbahn in Austria is not much of a town. It has a famous railway museum, a few guest-houses and a dark past that its 9,000-odd residents avoid mentioning to the tourists who pass through it. It was here, in a brutal concentration camp, that Adolf Eich-mann, the supreme logistician of the Nazi Holocaust, incarcerated 21,000 Hungarian Jews towards the end of the war, hostages to a regime that had already dispatched millions in the extermination camps of Poland.

The inmates of the Strasshof camp were the lucky ones: most of them managed to survive the war as slave labourers in the factories and workshops of nearby Vienna. The locals – like most Austrians who, after 1945, tended to suffer a collective amnesia about the Nazi regime and their part in it – prefer to talk about the *Sound of Music* scenery, the beer and the flowers of this 'garden city' suburb of the capital rather than their association with victims and tormentors. 'It's all in the past now,' said one elderly resident shortly after his town marched into the history books again at 12.53 p.m. on the sunny afternoon of 23 August 2006.

At that precise moment a young, pale, frightened woman, her skin ghostly white after years of being kept away from natural light, her eyes squinting and watery from the sunshine that she was so unused to, made a run from the driveway of No. 60 Heinestrasse. She dropped a Bosch vacuum cleaner that she had been using to clean the inside of a BMW car, and ran.

There were no searchlights trained on her, no border guards with guns or dogs, no razor wire or death strips to negotiate. But this was nonetheless a great escape, a triumph of the human spirit over an unspeakable cruelty that had been visited on this waiflike teenager for the previous 3,096 days.

This was the moment that a ten-year-old girl had dreamed of since she had been snatched from a street on her way to school by the kind of man parents warn their children about, a predator of the sort that Hollywood scriptwriters and imaginative novelists invent to represent evil incarnate. But what happened to her was no fiction, and there were many times during her imprisonment when she doubted whether the story of her life would ever have a happy ending.

The man who had robbed this young woman of her childhood, placing her life in suspension to satisfy the strange demons which drove him, had turned his back on her momentarily to answer a call on his mobile telephone. That distraction, that split instant in which God seemed to send a message that he had not forgotten

Natascha Kampusch, was the impetus to set her running to free herself from a captivity which by its nature and length would later, by turns, both stun and baffle the world.

She had little time. She had to use those first seconds – as the vacuum cleaner still buzzed on the floor of her captor's BMW 850i car and housewives in neighbouring homes cooked their midday meals – to put distance between her and the man who had stolen her life. The last time she had known freedom like this was as she walked to school on the blustery and wet morning of 2 March 1998, before vanishing into the clutches of the psychotic Wolfgang Priklopil.

Muscles unused to exercise, powered by the twin engines of fear and adrenalin, pumped her undernourished body as she scrambled over hedges, through back gardens and into a neighbouring street. It was a 200-metre dash that was not captured on camera. Had it been, it would have been a defining photographic moment . . . the moment she chose a better life. Later she would describe the decision to flee as spontaneous:

> I just knew that if not then, then maybe never. I looked over at him. He had his back to me. Just moments before then I had told him that I couldn't live like that any more. That I would try to escape. And well, I thought, if not now . . .
>
> For me it was like an eternity, but in reality it was 10 or 12 minutes. I simply ran into the allotment area, I jumped over many fences. In a panic I ran in a circle, to

see if there were any people anywhere. First I rang on the doorbell of this house but for some reason that didn't work, then I saw there was something happening in the kitchen.

I had to be very clear and explicit that this was an emergency. As taken aback as this woman was, she would not have reacted straight away. She kept saying, 'I don't understand, I don't understand.' Again and again she said that. 'I don't understand all this.'

She didn't let me in. For a split second that amazed me. But to let a complete stranger into your apartment – you have to also understand this woman, in that little house with a sick husband. I couldn't allow myself to even hide behind a bush. I was afraid that the criminal would kill this woman, or me, or both of us.

That's what I said. That he could kill us. The woman was still really worried and didn't want me to step on her tiny piece of lawn. I was in shock. What I really didn't want was for a local police car from the nearby Gänserndorf office to come. I wanted straight away to talk to the person in charge of the 'Natascha Kampusch Case'.

Two policemen came. I said that I had been kidna— well, that I ran away and that I had been kept imprisoned for eight years. They asked me what my name was and when I was born and where and which address and so on. I told them all that. Naturally that wasn't all that great. Then they repeated the information I gave them into their radios. I then basically insisted that they walk in one line together with me to their car. I'm not simply walking through this garden to the car, I told them.

And so the officers checked with their superiors and a child who detectives had long listed as dead had been reborn as a young woman – frightened and uncertain but safe, finally freed from the clutches of a man who gave her gifts one day and threatened to kill her the next, if she should ever try to flee from him.

Hours later Wolfgang Priklopil was dead, propelled to throw himself under the wheels of a Vienna train by the impending shame and the punishment that was about to befall him. It robbed the world of the chance to see justice done in a court of law: it also meant that the complexity of their captive-captor relationship could only ever be explained by her.

And explanations are still needed. It emerged within days of this spectacular grand finale, as each jet landing at Vienna international airport brought more reporters and TV camera crews, as the fax machines of her lawyers overheated with offers of contracts for interviews, movies and TV rights spewing out on to the floor, that the relationship forged in the dungeon he constructed for her, and in the outings that he took her on, was far from the simple slave and master, victim and oppressor, good versus evil saga that a spellbound world wanted to believe.

That it was a crime of grotesque proportions to steal a child from her loved ones can never be denied. But the situation developed at No. 60 Heinestrasse during her years of captivity and gradually Natascha seems to have become to some extent the manipulator of Priklopil, to have shrewdly mastered his emotions to gain modicums of freedom, material things and even affection. Some newspapers, perhaps unfairly, have latched on to this and portrayed her as the 'hostage from hell'. As a result, less than four weeks after she was snatched, Austrian newspapers and Internet sites were being deluged with hate mail from people claiming she was not a victim but a willing guest – one whose DNA may have been found in his bed (someone's other than his own was discovered and it is known that he never had a girlfriend) and asking why she never tried to escape earlier despite what appear to have been repeated chances to do so.

Relationships, like life, are never simple. Things occurred under the roof of No. 60 Heinestrasse that only two people knew about, and one of them took their secrets to the grave. This book seeks to answer the questions that Natascha has so far chosen not to answer. In doing so, it passes no judgement on her. It does, however, attempt to solve the riddle of what has become the most spellbinding human interest story of the decade – we ask why him, why her, and what happened to turn a coldhearted kidnapping into something approaching a love story.

The authors have been following this story since Natascha Kampusch was first kidnapped in 1998, and we have unique access to investigators probing the intricate details of the case. So without denying the astonishing power of Natascha's own story, nor indeed her incredible personal heroism, we have been digging, and continue to dig, into areas that could yet give a new perspective to this most amazing drama.

Did her family know the kidnapper, even as a passing acquaintance? Just how unhappy was Natascha as a child? Was the cellar a place of comfort, a refuge from a home fractured by rowing and separation? What was the 'tenderness' that bloomed between Natascha and her captor? Did she have opportunities to escape before she actually fled?

Did she, in other words, choose to remain?

It is a story quite unlike any other the world has known, with concluding details yet to be written by Natascha herself. But this work will attempt to give readers enough information to conclude for themselves if this case should be seen in black and white, or in the many shades of grey that complicate the emotions naturally triggered by what took place. Things are seldom as they seem in this incredible story.

I

A Difficult Childhood

Vienna. A city of romance, of suspense, of intrigue, history and glory. The imperial heart of the Habsburgs, the setting for Graham Greene's masterly post-war thriller *The Third Man*, the city of the not-so-blue Danube, Strauss waltzes and cream cakes that seem to make one put weight on simply by staring at them. It lures visitors from all over the world throughout the year and hosts important global organisations, such as the International Atomic Energy Agency and various UN bodies. These are what the visitor knows, the grand buildings of times past are what they see; the boiled beef and Sacher Torte cakes are what they eat. There was never a reason to spoil a holiday with a walk to the dismal 22nd district, where Vienna becomes less of a *grande dame* and more a pockmarked old hag.

The area is now called Donaustadt (Danube town), in a bid by the city authorities to sever the sinkhole housing estates and decrepit industrial areas from their old reputation, but a name change alone cannot lift the miasma of despair that hangs over much of this area. Tower blocks where up to 25 per cent of the inhabitants are jobless, public areas where addicts shoot up and drunks brawl, fall over, fight again and fall asleep, menacing half-lit walkways of tenements where predators offer drugs or sex or both – these were not what the average visitor to Vienna wanted to put on the itinerary. But the 22nd district is on the must-see map now, destined to become a magnet for ghouls, crime enthusiasts and the merely curious. Like the 'grassy knoll' in Dallas, where conspiracy theorists put the second gunman involved in the assassination of JFK, or the underpass in Paris where Princess Diana died, it generates its own aura for a world spellbound by what happened to a little girl who grew up here. Taxis regularly come to the Rennbahnweg estate and pull up outside apartment block No. 38, that houses flat No. 18. The driver winds down the window and points, and his passengers stare, following his finger as it traces an arc in the sky towards the seventh floor. Sometimes they just click a camera; sometimes they step outside to sniff the air, clamber back inside and are gone, their curiosity sated. Now they can tell their friends, when poring over the holiday snaps, 'That's where she lived, you know.'

This is the touchstone of victimhood, the place where Natascha Kampusch was born on 17 February 1988 and grew up to fulfil her peculiar, unique appointment with history.

Her home was part of one of the huge social housing blocks built by the left-wing government of Vienna in the post-war reconstruction years. The building has more than 2,400 apartments and 8,000 residents. The area she ended up in, by contrast, was designed as a garden suburb for the city's well-to-do.

The story of Natascha could begin with the Brothers Grimm formula of 'Once upon a time', because, once upon a time, life was good for her father and mother. Ludwig Koch, a 24-year-old master baker – thrifty, industrious, solid, respectable – fell in love with attractive divorcee Brigitta Sirny, 29, mother to two daughters. The year was 1980 and Ludwig's business was expanding.

Things are very different now. Eight and a half years of coping with the catastrophic loss of his daughter and of his businesses – he had at one time a string of bakeries on the go – have taken their toll on Ludwig.

He drinks too much, and he seems both confused and saddened by the events of August 2006: overjoyed at an outcome he never dreamed of, while bitter at what he can see is an industry forming around his beloved Natascha – something which, like the forces which stripped him of love and work, he has no control over.

The relationship with Natascha's mother fell apart long before she was taken from their lives, but he has flashes of nostalgia, Kodak moments of tenderness for the woman he once loved. He told the authors in an exclusive interview:

I was never married to Natascha's mother. We were together about 13 years, and we lived together for between seven and eight years. I can't remember exactly, but it was about that long. We met through a mutual friend, who introduced us to each other and it just went from there. We got on really well at the start and we had a business together – she came to work in the bakery. It was a joint decision to have a baby. She was planned and wanted by both of us. It was our dream to have a family, although Natascha's mother already had two children of her own.

My daughter was born in the Goettlicher Heiland hospital on the Hernalser Hauptstrasse. It was a wonderful moment. I can't remember how long the birth lasted, I think it was for four or five hours. I remember that before I'd been really happy about the pregnancy as the baby was a real planned and wanted thing, but I had been certain I would have a son. I had told everyone I would have a son and made bets, and when we found that it was a girl I was genuinely shocked, but when I held her in my arms for the first time my heart just melted. I knew I would not have changed her for the world. She was just perfect in every way. I was there for the birth, which I suppose for blokes of my generation is a bit different.

We called her Natascha because of my father, also called Ludwig. He had survived five years in a Russian jail after being captured by the Soviets in the war, and when he came back we would always joke about the Russian women, and I called her Natascha for him. I always loved the name anyway.

He died in 1988, but held Natascha in his arms before

he died. He was 80 when he passed on, so he had a full life. He was also a master baker like me, that's why I went into the business. He was healthy right up to the last and died of a heart attack. I am happy he saw her before his death. Sadly my mother, Anna, died two years ago, so she didn't live to see Natascha found. Anna and Natascha were very close – she was her favourite grandmother.

Natascha is my only child. Some people say that they can understand how hard it was to have lost my only child, but it wouldn't have made any difference if I'd had a dozen other children. A child is a child, and the loss was terrible. I would not wish on anyone what I had to go through.

I don't really know where our relationship went wrong after Natascha was born, I don't want to analyse it other than to say both of us made failures. Probably it was more to do with the business we had together than anything else. I think money always causes so many arguments. The relationship ended suddenly when she changed the locks on the flat and I knew it was all over. I guess that was about four years before Natascha was taken. There was some discussion of the custody, and in the end it was agreed that I would have Natascha every second weekend. I don't think she was in the ideal place where she lived. That was nobody's fault – it just wasn't a great place for a child, and I wanted to do my best for her whenever I had her with me. I wanted every weekend to be a holiday, and I used to take her to Hungary with me. I had and still have a house near a thermal bath resort in Sarvar in western Hungary. Actually, the village where my house is is about eight kilometres outside, it is called Nyoger, and I think she loved it there.

She was with me all the time, wherever I went. If I went to a disco she went along, if I went to see a friend she came too. We were often swimming, most of the time in fact, and in the village she had loads of friends. Sometimes we went walking. I was convinced when she vanished that she was unhappy at home and had fled there, to Hungary, but that was not the case.

I got to know Hungary because I was often there with my work as a master baker. I advised Hungarian factories. There were a lot of Austrians living there. Natascha was hugely popular as always. She could talk to five people at the same time and keep them all entertained. She was learning Hungarian – children pick up foreign languages very quickly – and she always told me she wanted to be a translator when she got older. I think she has a gift for communication.

She always loved animals as a young girl. She had two cats in Vienna. One of them was called Cindy, and I still have her. But after my daughter was taken, my mother said I should re-name the cat Natascha, because that would bring good luck – nine lives and all that. So we called her Tashy.

Her room was full of dolls as well, I know she had a lot, loads of them given to her by all her family, she always loved dolls. She loved music, especially Herbert Groenemeyer [Germany's most famous pop singer].

As a child she was always very grown-up; when other children might have been more interested in fairy tales, she was fascinated by watching the news. She was always reading books that could give her facts and figures about the world around her. The books she liked to read were those that broadened her horizons. I know she liked books about natural history. I know when she was in that cellar she spent a lot of time alone and she had to learn to keep herself amused. Documentaries and books that kept her informed about the world were her passion.

I found out Natascha was missing when her mother called me that day. To be honest I wasn't really that worried – I knew they had had a row, because Natascha's mother told me. I thought she was just trying to scare her mother, and I wasn't really worried about it until the next day when she still hadn't turned up. Then the nightmare started.

I have been through hell, but my life has really changed now. I have a new wife and now I have my daughter back. I'm 51 years old and I'm still young enough to enjoy my time with both. There is a very famous song by Udo Juergens with a line that goes 'The sun always shines'. That is my motto for my life.

I remember in Hungary how happy she was when one of the neighbours invited her to help them make marmalade, and they made a jar for her to take home with her. She was so proud.

Love and pride radiate from Ludwig Koch for his child, that is evident. But life was not rosy for the young

Natascha, not before she was taken, and certainly not afterwards. She lived on a dreary estate in a flat that was often empty after her parents broke up. Her two half-sisters were grown-ups now and lived away, and there was, and still is, an aura of the downtrodden among the residents. To them, life's glittering prizes seemed destined for other, luckier folk. Not people like her.

Neighbours who still live there say the tensions that existed between the parents were passed along to Natascha, who expressed them in the classical ways of children uncertain of themselves or their world: bed wetting, anxiety, low self-esteem and oscillating weight. By the time she was taken she endured a cruel nickname among her classmates: Porky. She had put on 10 kilos in just two months before she was snatched.

She was, like the man she would share her formative years with, not brilliant at school, whatever her parents say. She had above-average intelligence but was an average student: indeed the fact she was snatched while on her way to school earlier than usual came about because she needed extra tuition in German. She was regarded as a pretty, charming girl by neighbours and the mothers of her school friends, but nothing marked her out as extraordinary. She was good at handicrafts, and at kindergarten, when she was four, she made a clay figurine that her father keeps to this day.

The Alt Wien (Old Vienna) kindergarten on Leopold-auerplatz 77 in Vienna's 21st district, where Natascha went after school, is only two minutes' walk away from the Brioschiweg Volksschule, where she was a pupil.

Josefine Huttarsch is headmistress of the kindergarten, where she has worked for the past 30 years. She smiled at the mention of Natascha and spoke very fondly of her:

I remember Natascha very well, although I have not seen her for so many years. She was a very bright child, very aware of things, and very aware of herself in a way. And she definitely was immensely self-confident and cocky, but in a nice way. She was a nice girl, we never had any problems with her.

The children in this kindergarten are up to ten years old and they come here because their parents work long hours. They do their homework for school here and Natascha was always good at doing that. Of course, sometimes she would spend more time playing and then not have too much time left for the homework, but that's normal.

She liked to draw and play creative games a lot, as far as I can remember, I think she also liked sculpting with plasticine. She also was a very lively little girl, ran around the whole time and liked playing outdoors in the garden.

She had been spending lot of time with grown-ups, I think, with neighbours and friends of the parents, and was therefore able to make conversation like an adult. I think she matured quite early due to the circumstances of her parents not living together and her having frequent contact with adults.

She was very witty and liked to make jokes, and got along well with everyone. I remember she spoke properly even at a very young age – she was a very articulate child. She had many friends and was always playing with the other children. She was not one to sit alone in a corner.

But at times there was some sadness in her, I don't really know how to explain it, it was nothing overt, but there were times like that. I think that she might have had a hard time at home, with her parents separating and all. At the time I didn't think about it much, because many children coming from a similar background face the same problems and it is more or less normal.

But she was very impulsive too. Sometimes she would have big arguments with her mum when she was picking her up. She usually came and went by herself, because her school is just around the corner, but her mother would come to pick her up in the afternoons sometimes. I remember them having arguments as they were leaving, and voices would be raised too.

But it did not strike me as something worrying – you see that kind of stuff all the time. I assumed she had some problems at home, but it did not really show when she was with us in the kindergarten. She never mentioned anything directly.

Natascha also argued with her dad sometimes – nothing really serious – when he would be late to pick her up. She was very stubborn and quite wilful, but of course not in a bad way.

I remember very well the last day she was with us, it was a Friday. She was full of energy on that day, even more than usual. Her father was picking her up and taking her to Hungary over the weekend, and she was a bit upset that he was late. She wasn't cross with him or anything, she just could hardly wait for him to finally show up. Her dad was often a bit late when he was supposed to pick her up, but that's because he worked a lot. But Natascha was always looking forward to the trips to Hungary.

Natascha was close to stepsisters Claudia, born in 1968, and Sabine, born in 1970, and is now an aunt several times over, but they could do little to protect her from the feelings of alienation she must have felt. Rows between her parents upset the sensitive Natascha. She loved them both, but neighbours tend to think she was more of a daddy's girl. And there are allegations that Frau Sirny often left Natascha on her own, fuelling resentments with each passing day.

Experts have long warned of the potential negative effects of parents arguing in front of their children. A recent study, by the University of Rochester in New York, said it is not only the obvious stuff – throwing objects, shouting and swearing – that distresses children, but also the more subtle, simmering resentment practised by families who pride themselves on never fighting in front of the children.

Penny Mansfield, the director of the marriage and partnership organisation One Plus One, says: 'Parents who are distracted by their own conflict tend to be less good at parenting. The children don't get enough attention.' Another way some children react, she says, is to mimic the rows they witness. 'They learn that this is how you relate to people. But most potentially destructive is when the child thinks: "If Dad is so angry at Mum, he can be that angry at me." Their security is threatened.'

Ludwig admits there were rows, admits there was tension, but he claims no knowledge of whether it was destructive to Natascha. He hopes not, he says. He has found happiness with his new wife Georgina, 48, a Hungarian schoolteacher, and now lives in a house in the same district where he once lived with Natascha and Brigitta. He inherited it but had to sell it, and now pays rent to live there, the legacy of the business that he lost in the wake of Natascha's kidnap.

'What else can I tell you about her?' he says, racking his memory. 'She was a very intelligent and creative child. I remember at the age of ten she could already command the full attention of over six adults around her. She would simply talk and talk, entertain everyone and make them laugh. She was a real chatterbox, very extrovert and communicative from a very early age.

'She had many friends in the neighbourhood and in school. She loved going to school and I think she did well there, too. She liked all of her subjects.'

He said that one of her big joys was the kitten she had been given shortly before she was stolen.

With so much time at home alone she spent a lot of time with the cat and really loved it. It was still young when she vanished. We had a much older cat that had belonged to my mother, it was called Muschi I think, and it had kittens and we gave Natascha one of the kittens. She was delighted, and she raised it by feeding it milk from a bottle.

Hannes Bartsch, the owner of the Planet Music in Vienna, was a pal in Hungary. He gets all the big rock groups to his place. Natascha met some of them when he brought them down to Hungary. She liked rock music. You know, when I was doing better financially, had a better life, we were down at the Woerthersee, oh, five or six times a year. [The Woerthersee is a favourite vacation resort, catering to more affluent Austrians, set in magnificent mountain scenery in Carinthia.]

They were filming a famous Austrian TV series when we were there, *Ein Schloß am Woerthersee* ['A Castle by Lake Woerther'], and Natascha got to meet the cast. She was friendly with the stars, Roy Black and Franco Adolfo. They were regulars in the hotel I stayed in. All the stars went there, she experienced all this when she was a little kid. She would talk to them and was never shy. That's why today she is not afraid of big names and the spotlight, it was nothing special to her.

Back to the present, and he is keen to show off something. Rising from the table as if wanting to somehow share those precious moments, he walks from his small, wood-panelled kitchen into the garden, shading his eyes from the sunlight as he rummages for the key to the shed. He then pulls open the doors and wheels an electric car out on to the brick yard. 'Of course when Natascha was here this yard was grass, some things change, but I have always kept her car for her. The batteries are flat now, but I have always kept it clean for her,' he says and, as if emphasising the point, pulls a handkerchief from his pocket and uses it to brush a fleck from the bonnet.

Down the long years of her captivity this car had become a touchstone of faith when despair was all around. After the long nights tramping the more sordid areas of Vienna, he would come back to this toy that his lost daughter loved so much. It seemed that just by touching it he could summon her spirit back.

What it cost was not important. Sometimes things went well with my businesses and sometimes things didn't go well. Life is like that, a roller-coaster, but what was always important for me was that I did my best for my child.

And I didn't just give her presents. I also tried to give her good advice and warn her about life. I always told her to stay away from false friends, from people who just say yes because they want something from you. They show a friendly face but they just want to stick a knife in your back. That's a lesson she still has with her today, as a lot of people want something from her.

He said Natascha was never a materialistic child, and would shun fancy presents in favour of more practical ones. He recalled the time on one Hungarian trip when he took her to buy some 'nice fancy shoes':

But she only glanced though the shelves and went straight to the far corner of the shop and picked a pair of Wellington boots. She didn't care about the fancy shoes, she only wanted wellies so she could play in the garden, water the lawn and the flowers and things like that. She loved playing in the garden and the outdoors in general.

Natascha is so much like my mother, the resemblance is incredible. She has her looks, her spirit, her intelligence. When I was watching the interview on TV, it was as if I was looking at my late mother when she was younger.

But Natascha's got the will to fight from me, and the stubbornness, too. That's why she could endure everything and that is why she is now able to take control over her own fate.

It was while she was on holiday in Hungary shortly before she was kidnapped that Natascha came closest to puppy love. Martin Bartsch, 21, son of her father's friend Hannes, said he thought of her as a 'little girlfriend', and recalled how, even though she was three years younger than him, a big gap at the time, he enjoyed her company:

She wasn't a typical girl of her age. Usually I found them annoying, but Natascha was interesting to talk to and polite. We would go cycling all around the area. There was a football pitch we used to like to stop at – I was mad about football and always wanted to kick the ball about – and she would always join in, although I don't know how much she liked football. But that's what she was like, always willing to join in with everything.

We never used to take food with us, we went home for that, usually at my place, as my mother was there and Natascha liked her a lot. I never saw Natascha's mum in Hungary. She was only ever there with her dad. I know he was a great cook, obviously, especially with the bakery stuff, but I think he likes just to rest at the weekends and get away from it all. But you could see he loved Natascha a lot, they had a great relationship, and he was really considerate and caring about her. When we had the grill evenings, sometimes there would be five people there and sometimes there would be 15, but it was always the same.

When Natascha wasn't playing she would be cuddling her dad. I think he was the most important player in the whole search for her. He never gave up. Everyone else I'm sure believed she would never be seen again – I didn't think I would ever see her again. But her dad never for a second wavered in his belief that he would one day find his Natascha.

Natascha's last day of freedom before her ordeal began was spent in Hungary with her father and the Bartsch family. They shared a meal together, which was late coming to the table, making them late in turn getting back to Vienna and triggering the row that was to have such catastrophic consequences.

It was a meal where everyone sat around 'laughing and talking', according to Erika Bartsch, Hannes's wife. Natascha had spent the morning playing with the Bartsch family sheepdog and the early afternoon picking plums from her garden to make jam. She is remembered as a child especially fond of nature, who loved butterflies and enjoyed the nature trails which criss-crossed the region. She liked climbing trees, stroking the heads of the horses in a nearby meadow and, in wintertime, took special delight in sledging on nearby hills. The absence of nature, of the seasons themselves, when she was a prisoner in his dungeon, must have been particularly hard for her to bear.

Sometimes she took a sewing kit with her on her weekends away and made clothes for her dolls. Often she would weave bracelets from grass and tell her hosts, 'I am making one to give to Mami.' She is remembered, above all, as the opposite of the man who would come to possess her: sociable, likeable, charming, kind and extrovert. Frau Bartsch recalled those happy days:

The kids would play football together on the pitch nearby, or go skipping or hopping, or else they were climbing in the trees. Right opposite us there was a path that led into the woods which was great for the cycles. It was a good life for them. They were forced to amuse themselves to a certain extent, because the other children were Hungarian and they only had a few words, so they couldn't really talk with each other.

When we had a barbecue the kids would play in the garden – we had 2,600 square metres – and we adults would sit and talk about everything under the sun. Natascha's mother never came there, she was always just there with her father. You could see she was happy and had a good relationship with him. Sometimes when she was tired she would sit on his knee and have a cuddle, they were very close.

Hungary was a kind of Narnia for Natascha, a never-ending holiday away from the dispiriting tower blocks and potholed streets where she lived. There was no one there to call her Porky or poke fun at her bed-wetting. In fact, according to her father, it stopped when she was there.

They were joyous episodes, which she cherished when in captivity, and her father hopes to take her back there soon to explore the haunts of a lost childhood.

A lost childhood indeed – and a childhood that perhaps had a darker side than the hours merely spent alone in her mother's flat or shut in her room while her parents argued. It was one exposed when police from Task Force Natascha were handed a set of four colour photographs of Natascha as a child. This was shortly after she disappeared. But these were shockingly different to those of Natascha at her first Communion, or the smiling school photographs that adorned the Missing posters pinned up around the city.

Almost naked, with thigh-length boots and a riding crop, and a tiny top that only reached part of the way to her stomach, she looks uncomfortable as she stares off to the left at the floor. In another she is naked on the bed, wrapped only in a fake fur stole.

The pictures were reluctantly handed over by

Natascha's mother after they were seen by someone close to the story from day one, who borrowed some of them and passed them on to the police and to an expert psychologist in child abuse. Speaking on condition of anonymity, the person who found the pictures told the authors:

> There were pictures of Natascha in a box of family snaps, and I was leafing through them as I chatted to Natascha's mother.
>
> I was shocked when I saw them, and asked her what they were, and she seemed embarrassed, and dismissed them as family snaps taken by Claudia. She had promised to let me have some pictures, so I asked for them. She refused, and so I asked her: 'What are they, harmless, or not harmless? If they are harmless, surely I can have them?'
>
> She agreed, but I could see she was uncomfortable. I gave them straight to police and an expert on child abuse, who immediately came back to say he was very concerned about them.
>
> But the police expert, Dr Max Friedrich, charged with leading the medical team looking after Natascha in the first weeks following her escape, said the pictures were not criminal.

Dr Eva Wolfram-Ertl, another psychiatric expert trained to aid child victims of sexual abuse, also saw the photographs. She said, unequivocally, that they showed a child of around five years of age and that they were sexual in nature. Dr Wolfram-Ertl said that she and her colleagues all agreed that these pictures 'left no room for interpretation.' As she told the top Austrian magazine *Profil* in 1998: 'Taking the pictures raises serious questions about sexual abuse. These poses, a small child wouldn't adopt such poses on their own. This is not about the child, her well-being, her development or her needs, it is just about the needs of the grown-up who certainly animated the child into such postures.'

According to Dr Wolfram-Ertl, children have their own eroticism and exhibitionistic phases in their development, but an act of abuse begins when adult persons with paedophile tendencies use children's sexuality for the satisfaction of their own perverse desires.

From a psychoanalyst's point of view, Dr Wolfram-Ertl said at the time that she would like to eliminate any link between the photographs and the disappearance of Natascha. Dr Wolfram-Ertl wanted a thorough investigation into any men who may have met Natascha, for example friends of her mother or father. She also mentioned Natascha's symptoms – wetting the bed, poor performance in school and the oscillating weight – as sometimes related to a sexualised atmosphere at home, which the photos suggested.

When contacted for this book about the remarks that put her at odds with one of Austria's most famous psychiatrists, Dr Wolfram-Ertl declined to comment further. Her interview at the time remains her sole analysis of the pictures.

As for Professor Friedrich, it was his expert opinion that her disappearance could not be connected to paedophile pornography that had stopped the police investigation from following this line of inquiry.

He was asked this question at a press conference shortly after Natascha was freed: 'Is it right that you have written an expert opinion in 1998 concerning her and her family surroundings? That in 1998, there was the assumption that within her family environment there might be sexual abuse? Is it right that you were dealing with that assumption in that expert opinion? And to which conclusion did you come?'

Professor Friedrich looked uncomfortable at the question and replied, 'I was working in a team of criminologists who served me with information. And I could also get information on my own.'

QUESTION: 'Which conclusion did you draw then?'
ANSWER: 'I don't know whether that report is still sealed by police. I will not give any comment. What is written in there were my thoughts.'

Claudia was never charged with any crime over the pictures, if indeed she did take them, as her mother claims. When contacted by the authors for confirmation, the family declined to comment. Several detectives who worked on the Natascha case down the years expressed themselves dumbfounded that these pictures could ever be regarded as innocent.

Max Edelbacher, 62, a former leader of the police squad that was assigned to hunt for her, who was interviewed for this book, classified Natascha as an abused child. He said:

Ninety-five per cent of all missing children cases are solved within 24 hours, when this hadn't happened in this case we called the mother in to interview.

She was well known as a woman that liked men. From the start of the investigation details of her relationships were quickly known. The men around her, particularly those who met Natascha, ought to have been properly investigated. An example of how the case was not properly investigated was in the failure to do a search of Natascha's home. It was a mistake not to follow this line more.

I know about the photographs, and that they were shown to Max Friedrich, but I believe he made a mistake in suggesting that should not be investigated further. I also think it was a mistake that he was the person that had responsibility for her care when she was found. I did speak to Claudia and she confirmed she had taken the photographs.

When Natascha was free and taken to the police station at Deutsch-Wagram they had her for maybe one or two hours, and I think this was the biggest mistake of all. This was the time when the matter could have been solved and the full truth known. Instead she was interviewed by policewomen in a station with officers who knew nothing about the case and had no idea what questions to ask. In addition the people who had taken over the case in 2002 had nothing to do with it before that date and were therefore not as well informed as the original team. If some of the original team had been given access to her in this crucial one or two hours we might have been able to clear up the mysteries that still surround this case. I'm not criticising officers in Burgenland but they do not have to deal with the level of crime in the capital city and if the Vienna officer from the original Natascha squad had been given access to her the situation might have been very different.

As it is Natascha now has her story and she is sticking to it. I don't know what went on in the conversations between her and Max Friedrich but I know that the police were not given proper access and her family were also barred. Instead she was counselled and the chance to get the full story was lost. She has been allowed to create her own version of events and there is no way anyone is going to get through that at any stage now. I think the best that we can hope for is that when she gets to at least 30 or older, some of the truth or the whole truth may finally come out, but now there is no chance.

We know that Natascha was abused by her mother's lover at the time, he used to shout at her and mistreated her, she used to tell others who we interviewed about it including her father. My wife was a teacher at the school and she told me that Natascha was definitely a strange child, clearly intelligent yet not performing as well as one might have expected and with a worldly wise attitude about her that was beyond her years.

Wenzel Schimanek, 56, and his wife Lotte still live on the same landing in the same tower block as Brigitta Sirny and used to baby-sit little Natascha when Sirny was away – which they claim was very often. Herr Schimanek, a lorry driver of Czech origin, is a very good friend of Ludwig Koch and meets regularly with him, for a beer, and to chat about old times. He was impressed by the young Natascha, as he told the authors:

Natascha was the most intelligent child I had ever seen. She was speaking all the time and entertained everyone around her. At the age of six she could have a real conversation with an adult person and always knew the answers to everything. We played cards with her when she was around five.

She was also very funny. She was a very witty child and was telling jokes all the time and making everyone laugh. She really was an adorable little girl.

She loved animals, she played with all the cats and dogs from the neighbourhood and had one cat of her own, Tashy, which still lives with Herr Koch. She loved watching TV, but was also often out and about playing with other children.

She used to draw a lot. She liked drawing and that sort of thing – she was very creative.

The Schimaneks used to go on weekend trips outside Vienna with Koch and Sirny and little Natascha, and they often went to neighbouring Hungary (but not to Koch's holiday house). Herr Schimanek recalled one of these trips:

> Once while we were in Hungary, Luki [Koch's nickname] told everyone he had a surprise for us. He got us on to this horse carriage and we went down this country road. He was just telling everyone about how interesting the surprise would be, when we came to a pool of water on the road in front of us. One of the horses tried to jump over it while the other simply stopped. That caused the axle of the carriage to break and the whole thing turned over.
>
> Luki reacted quickly and threw little Natascha on the grass, but the rest of us, including him, flipped over with the carriage into the pool of muddy water. We all ended up soaked and very dirty, and little Natascha started to laugh, shouting: 'This is your surprise, this is your surprise, what a funny surprise! Look at you!' We all had to laugh, standing there soaked and dirty in that pool of mud.

Schimanek moved on to say that two years before Natascha's disappearance Frau Sirny simply stopped talking to them for no apparent reason and they never found out why to this day. 'We were the best of neighbours,' he said, 'and friends too, but something happened and she stopped talking to us. We never found out why.'

But in the Wars of the Roses atmosphere that began to dominate life at flat 18, Natascha increasingly found herself caught in the middle of a disintegrating relationship. Ironically, it was the skills that she would learn while vying for the affections of her parents that would stand her in good stead when captive.

Neither Frau Sirny nor Natascha has said whether the slap she received across the face on the day she walked into captivity was an isolated incident: experts think not. Frau Sirny admitted she felt a little bad about it, but at the same time she said that children need 'discipline'. Natascha herself has since dismissed it as little more than a 'clip' and not something she dwelled on.

Frau Sirny never gave any indication that this was the only time it happened. A slap is a long away from systemised brutality, but there seemed to be an environment surrounding Natascha unconducive to healthy development: rowing parents, rows with her mother, her mother often absent for long periods in the evenings, her unhappiness with her mother's choice of boyfriends. Natascha built up unseen walls, hidden defence mechanisms, within herself.

Natascha took into that cellar survival skills which she had learned at home, and which would enable her not only to get through the ordeal, but to master it.

'How you survive an extreme situation depends on what you know before you go into it,' wrote one commentator: a small phrase among the millions that have been penned about her since the story broke. The writer went on: 'Natascha survived because she already knew that people could be nasty; it wasn't a shock to her. She didn't have friends, she was lonely and unhappy, and by the time she was kidnapped she was already experienced in looking after herself.'

Experts discussing child–mother relationships talk of three different types of mothering figure. There is the always-reliable, all-loving, all-forgiving type; the one who is always horrible, and one who is a little of both – with the horridness usually being a child's take on discipline that he or she doesn't care for.

'That was the relationship Natascha had to form with her kidnapper, Wolfgang Priklopil. It appears that she had already had that kind of relationship with her parents, so she would have been skilled in making the most out of when he was nice, and dealing with him when he was nasty,' wrote one UK clinical psychiatrist from reading media reports. 'It would have been worse if she had had an entirely loving mother. Her kidnapper treated her as being special, and this gave her the loving, kindly attention that she had not always got from her parents.'

Since her release many experts have commented that they don't consider Natascha as a 'people person', and this gels with recollections of contemporaries who last saw her when she was in their class at school. 'She looks even more in control now than she wanted to be back then,' carped one. Control: it is the classic grail quested after by children who feel they have none.

Brigitte Weber, a lady who entered into a relationship with Ludwig after his long liaison with Natascha's mother ended, knew Natascha from several trips to Hungary and also had her to stay at her home in Vienna. She said Natascha had a strong bond with her eldest daughter and kept in touch via telephone with them after the relationship with Ludwig ended.

Frau Weber recalled what happened when an eight-year-old Natascha spent yet another weekend with her while Brigitta Sirny holidayed in Paris. She expressed a desire to stay with Frau Weber for good rather than returning home. She said that Natascha always looked for physical contact while they were watching TV, cuddling up to her, always wanting to be held, to be close, often sitting on her lap 'until my knees hurt'. She added: 'She said she wasn't allowed to do that with her mother because she was concerned that her clothes would wrinkle.'

Furthermore, Natascha claimed that her mother prohibited her from answering the phone when she was home alone, out of fear that the caller might realise that Natascha was unsupervised at an early age. According to Frau Weber, Natascha asserted that she often pretended to be sleeping when her mother left the house. When alone, Natascha often felt scared and 'received comfort from neighbours through the letter-box slit because Frau Sirny had forbidden her to open the door'.

Anneliese Glaser, the neighbour with whom Natascha spent several hours during her last night of freedom, is also scathing about Frau Sirny's qualities as a mother. It is unknown whether in the past huge rows engulfed these former friends, whether jealousies or hatreds drive her assessment of her. But her comments go to the heart of what others have said: Natascha was not a happy child. She told the authors:

Frau Sirny always complained about Natascha, she always spoke of her as if she was a problem child, but that was not the case at all. But Natascha never spoke badly of her mum, although we knew that she had a hard time with her.

Once Natascha stormed into the shop where I was working and hugged me and held me tightly for a minute. Then her mother came in, all red in the face and angry. When Natascha raised her head I saw that her eyes were all wet and her cheek was bright red – there was a hand imprint on it.

Natascha often spoke of her dad and her grandma, she really enjoyed the time with them and loved going there. She had a great relationship with her dad and her grandma, but the mother couldn't stand that.

I was so happy when the news about her escape broke. It was one day before my birthday, and I went to Herr Koch to celebrate with him, we were all so happy.

But I believe the whole truth has not been revealed yet.

The psychiatric experts have not only had a field day with the mind of the man who took Natascha, but also with Natascha herself.

Professor Johann Zapotoczky, head of the child and adolescent psychiatry clinic in Graz, said:

She was abducted at the age of ten, and by then her personality was already formed. She already knew about the world. If she came from a happy and loving family background, as she said in the interview, then she would have had a healthy foundation, an emotional basis on which to build a strong personality.

But even if the opposite was the case, she would have been ready to deal with her hardship in some way: if her previous circumstances were hard, that means she would have learned how to deal with difficult situations and how to interact with adults in that sense. In a way, if she had to deal with hardship before the abduction, it would mean she was prepared for what came after that.

Dr Reinhard Haller, Austria's most famous criminal psychiatrist, had this to say:

From what we hear and read, she was used to suffering from an early age and she developed ways to cope with that suffering. It seems she was exposed to violent behaviour as a child already and she had developed strategies of dealing with situations like that. Those survival strategies were obviously of great use to her during the years of captivity. A person who was, so to speak, hardened , who knew how to deal with extreme situations and who had experienced violence in early childhood but learned to cope with it, is obviously more prepared for an ordeal of any sort than any other person.

This was the life of Natascha Kampusch as seen through the eyes of those who knew her and those who would come to know her: the family, neighbours, friends and, finally, psychiatric experts tasked with reliving past trauma to build a happier future. Hers was not the best of worlds, although she had happy times in it. She over-ate, she wet the bed, her friends taunted her at school, she felt insecure.

It is possible, though, that her – albeit short – life experience had equipped her better than many children to survive the ordeal to come and that she would have been able to take from the trauma small day-to-day compensations, such as routine and attention, which made the horror bearable.

2

Wolfgang Priklopil: Portrait of a Monster?

In a land of curtain twitchers and neighbourhood snoops, forever ringing up the taxman to inform on the jobless resident across the way with his new car, writing indignant, anonymous letters to authorities about infractions real and perceived against the state, Wolfgang Priklopil never even registered on the radar. The famous Churchillian put-down of a political rival could easily have applied to him: he was a modest man, with much to be modest about.

Self-reliant, good with his hands and fastidious in his habits, he never drank, didn't smoke, didn't gamble and certainly had no time for women. Like some modern-day Norman Bates, the mad, mother-loving motel-keeper in Hitchcock's classic thriller *Psycho*, there was, outwardly at least, nothing major to signal to an unsuspecting world the strange demons which gripped him. He just seemed a bit of a mummy's boy, a nonentity, one whose dreams and fantasies were kept to himself. Many men have sexual fantasies, often dark and lurid ones. In the country where Freud was born, Priklopil could have satisfied his in cyberspace on any one of thousands of websites, or he could have paid for them to be acted out in the red-light zones of Vienna where money will buy most perversions with few questions asked or eyebrows raised.

His name has Czech roots and comes from a verb, the infinitive of which, 'pøiklopit', means 'to cover something'. 'Pøiklopil' is the past form of the verb, meaning that someone covered something.

Priklopil was an only child, and perhaps only two or three people really knew him, one of them being his mother: others he came into contact with saw the face he wished to present to them on any given day, in any given situation. He is described variously as 'a nice boy' – by his mother; as 'a reliable business partner', by the man who worked with him; as 'different', 'fogeyish', 'picky' and 'odd', by neighbours and work colleagues who never came close to divining the genuine article. No one ever said he was likeable, and perhaps that should be the epitaph on his unmarked grave: 'Here Lies an Unlikeable Man'.

At some point the loner who shared his life with cats, who doted on his mother, whose idea of a wild night was to read electronics magazines and technology journals, crossed the Rubicon from fantasy to reality and began to convert a cellar into a customised subterranean dungeon. If only those good neighbours in Heinestrasse, with their swimming pools and pristine barbecue patios, had looked beyond the lace curtains, or nurtured suspicions about whether he worked on the black market, Priklopil's obsession could have been thwarted before it began.

But they didn't and his apparent normality allowed him to commit a horrifying crime.

On 14 May 1962, Juan Carlos of Spain married the Greek Princess Sophia in Athens. Across the Atlantic, civil rights protestors in America marked the first anniversary of a bus firebombing in Alabama with a candle-lit vigil, while in Yugoslavia the former vice-president Milovan Djilas was given further jail time for publishing a book about Soviet leader Josef Stalin.

In Austria Wolfgang Priklopil was born into obscurity in the same district in which a young girl with whom he shared his destiny would be born 26 years later. James Bond was saving the world in *Dr No*, and The Beatles were singing the song which could well have been written for Priklopil: 'Love Me Do'.

His father, Karl, worked as the local representative for the German concern of Scharlachberg, the third largest brandy maker in the country, selling it to restaurants, bars and liquor outlets in the region. His mother, Waltraud, was a housewife who worked part-time as a shop assistant. Described as a kind, quiet woman by all who remember her, she was expected in bourgeois society to be a devotee of the three Ks of Austrian life: *Küche, Kinder und Kirche* – kitchen, children and church. It was a role she was said not to be unhappy with.

Not much is known about Karl, but one man with whom he forged a friendship has a tantalising piece of information that sheds light on the possible genesis of Wolfgang Priklopil's criminally deviant plan.

Heinrich Ehlers, born in Vienna in 1939 a Jewish Austrian, was best friends with Karl, and spent his first six years locked in a cellar. He said, 'When I saw the pictures on television of Wolfgang it was like looking at his father 20 years before. They were identical. When I heard what he had done my blood froze. It was uncanny. His father was fascinated by my story and he told me on one occasion: 'I told Wolfi about your life last night. He was spellbound, I can tell you!'

The Ehlers family including Heinrich's parents, grandmother and brother Eric, born in 1940, and sister Hermine, born in 1944, lived in two underground rooms just eight square metres in size separated by a glass panelled door, in the Margareten district of Vienna. Brought food by friends, they survived in this subterranean world until the end of the war.

Herr Ehlers went on, 'When I first saw the pictures of Natascha Kampusch I could empathise with her. I still suffer from bright light and I cannot bear to be in a confined space.' He trained as a mechanic at the Graef & Stift company where he met Karl. They were friends, he said, for 20 years, but he only ever met Wolfgang at Karl's funeral. When the story of the secret cellar hit the TV news bulletins, he said, 'what really shocked me were the pictures of this heavy safe door which he used to make the cellar secure. I started to have a panic attack. What would have happened to her if he had had a car crash? This girl must have been constantly in terror that one day he might never come back.'

* * *

The Priklopil family moved from their council flat at No. 30 Rugierstrasse to the Strasshof house in 1972 after the death of Wolfgang's grandfather Oskar. Karl inherited the 160 square metre house with four bedrooms and renovated it over the years. Wolfgang had a seemingly happy childhood, with the occasional family trip to the Italian Adriatic coast and other holidays spent on farms in Austria and Germany. There was an introspection to him, however, a solemnity punctuated by screaming fits with his mother, whom he adored but did not fear, and savage tongue-lashings from his father, who often scared him witless. His uncle, Johann, who lives in Heinestrasse next door to the Priklopil house, is understood to have tried to be a mediator between the young Wolfgang and his father – but he has refused all requests to speak about his disgraced, deceased nephew.

His parents used to worry about his lack of school friends. He was happiest reading in his room or completing huge jigsaw puzzles of famous structures like the Eiffel Tower. He also liked model-making and plastic aircraft kits. Toy trains were another passion: a supreme irony, given how his life would ultimately end. Essentially, he was into all kinds of solitary pursuits that kept him separate from his peers.

In school he was a middling student with average grades, although he always scored the highest marks in *Betragen* – behaviour. He was the kind of obedient student teachers pray for, even if his academic prowess was less than stellar. He went to Hauptschule Afritschgasse for four years until the age of 14. In the Austrian education system a Hauptschule is a cross between elementary and high school: his placement there meant he was neither at the top of the academic pile nor at the bottom, just an average kid in an average school.

But as he grew there were disturbing signs, ones that experts often use to determine whether simple anti-social behaviour or rebelliousness has the potential to lead to psychopathy. Cruelty to animals is one of them, fire-starting another, prolonged bed-wetting the third. He was guilty of the first and suffered the third into his late teens.

When he was 13, the technically gifted Priklopil, who scored high marks in metalworking and science at school, built his own air rifle, which he used to kill sparrows and pigeons in the back garden of the family home. He also took pot-shots at stray dogs, but cats were out of bounds. He had a respect for their solitary, predatory ways, and often would try to merely injure a bird so he could then sit, contentedly eating cake that his mother had baked for him, and wait and watch as a cat came along to toy with the wounded creature before finally killing it.

One neighbour who did not want to be named said: 'Sometimes you could hear the mother yelling at him – to do his homework, clean his room, take his clothes down to the washing machine.' There's nothing odd, of course, in the truculence of teenage children leading to an escalation in pitch and tone during arguments with their parents. 'But he would scream back at her, literally scream, that he was fed up being ordered about, that one day he would be in charge, and she would listen up then,' added the neighbour. 'It was always around lunchtime, when the father wasn't there: I think he was a little bit afraid of the father. And on the couple of occasions I heard them shouting – once when I was walking past to go to the shops – I heard her saying he should take his "wet bed things" to the washing machine before going out.' The same neighbour went on:

> Karl had set his mind on a son that I think he wanted to take to football, on hikes, to do 'manly' things with, but his son was sensitive and shy. There was friction too between Karl and Waltraud. He drank – he always had lots of free samples from his company, I saw him often unloading them from his car – and this was another flashpoint. Waltraud was very abstemious: a glass of hot wine at Christmas. So many of us never see beneath the surface of relationships and lives, like we never saw beneath the surface of his building and the secret underneath. It must be that something in his relationship with his parents made him what he was, mustn't it?

A school photograph of Priklopil at 14 shows an earnest-looking boy with dark eyes and thick hair parted on one side. It gives little clue as to what was going on inside his disturbed head. He wore the mask of innocence.

'I once told him he looked like a girl, he was so angelic-looking,' said Rosi Doni, a 55-year-old hairdresser who regularly cut his hair at the home he shared with his mother until 15 years ago. 'He liked it long and would never let me take off that much.' She recalls Priklopil's mother complaining that her son was obsessed with technology and that just getting into the family's house in Strasshof was 'a real effort'. 'I remember, after he had grown up and he was living with her alone there, the mother having to yell at me, saying, "Wait while I de-activate the security system so I can open the door."

'The house looked very normal, I can't remember anything peculiar about it, it was nice and tidy. The only thing I was surprised about is that he never spoke about girls, not once. And he was such a handsome man. He also looked a lot younger than he was.'

Long before Wolfgang the master pupated from Wolf-gang the servant, he began learning the skills which would enable him to indulge his fantasy. He started work as an apprentice at Siemens, the German electro-nics giant, when he was 15, after dropping out of technical school after one year, at a wage of some £25 per week. It was a good job with a solid company, and one which his father urged him to take, although accord-ing to some accounts he wanted to stay on at school.

Contemporaries at Siemens say he completed his ap-prenticeship with good marks and was subsequently hired by the firm. One of his ex-colleagues from this period described him as 'not at all ostentatious. He joined in all those normal jokes we did, like hiding untraceable malfunctions in switches, or letting an electrolyte-capa-citor "explode" exactly when the instructor passed by. Apart from that we thought he must have derived from a wealthy family, because he always had money.'

Ernst Winter, a fellow apprentice, remembered Priklopil's obsession with cars when he was working at Siemens, describing him as a 'petrol head' who really only became animated when talking about machines, not his fellows. 'The other thing that stood out is how much time he took over everything,' said Winter. 'He was slow, but thorough. Very thorough.' Nothing in his demeanour or his manners gave any inkling to the strange obsession that he was carrying around inside him – to kidnap a girl and hold her hostage – but at the time when other lads his age were dancing and dating girls, or at the very least dreaming of dating them, he had formed views on the opposite sex indicating his warped persona. He told a friend that 'all girls are tarts' and added: 'They don't interest me. I want a partner who will understand when I want to be alone, who can cook well, is happy to be only a housewife, who looks good but does not consider looks important. I want a woman who will simply support me in everything I do.'

Kurt Kletzer, a Vienna psychotherapist who is working on a detailed study of Wolfgang Priklopil and his adolescent slide into the mind's danger zone, said it is possible now that his school or family doctor might have picked up on his problems. 'But in the 1960s and early 70s being a quiet lad who liked to shoot birds wouldn't necessarily have marked him down as being a potential threat to other humans,' he said. 'But even then, there is not much beyond monitoring and medicating that could have been done. His mental make-up was formed. Probably, at best, society could have hoped merely to keep

Wolfgang Priklopil at bay. 'Was he a genuine psychopath genetically hard-wired to act as he did or was he a neurotic and a victim of the environment that raised him?'

Psychopathy is a term derived from the Greek psych (mind) and pathos (suffering), and was once used to denote any form of mental illness. These days, psychopathy is defined in psychiatry as a condition characterised by 'lack of empathy or conscience, poor impulse control and manipulative behaviour'.

It is unclear at what stage in his life his obsession to kidnap and detain a young girl for his pleasure developed. Naturally it has drawn parallels with Frederick Clegg, the strange and withdrawn 'collector' of the John Fowles book of the same name who, no longer content with butterflies, 'collects' art student Miranda Grey – he is fixated on her – and keeps her captive in his Sussex house. Fowles's compelling psychological study charts a battle of minds and wills which, in addition to its fascinating and terrifying account of a psychopath, lays open to display the powerful condition of attachment.

There is a common trait among psychopaths and neurotics – the need to hide things or characteristics in order to appear normal. Marc Dutroux, the Belgian paedophile, built himself the same kind of underground dungeon that he needed to carry out his crimes as Priklopil. Certainly his relationship to his father – and more significantly to his mother – made him the creature he became.

'I subscribe to the theory he was actually more of a

neurotic than a psychotic personality,' said Kurt Kletzer in an interview for this book.

Was he psychotic with an inbuilt genetic need to behave as he did [Kletzer asks], or was he a neurotic who was forced by the society and the world and the circumstances into which he was born to act as he did? I believe in his case it is the latter which played a greater role in making him what he was.

He has been called a kidnapper or criminal in all that has been written about him, but he was not born a kidnapper or criminal; a person can be born a duke or lord, but you are not born a kidnapper. There are some studies that indicate a genetic predisposition towards certain types of antisocial or criminal behaviour, but there are many people who may have these genetic traits who do not become kidnappers or criminals. What is vital to know in his case is what influenced him after he was born.

What role did genetics play, and what role did his upbringing play? What was his relationship to his mother and father?

What is certain is that there was something in his life which forced him to become detached from the real world and obsessed with his own inner world and a fantasy view of life. Typically it can be a very dominating father or a clinging mother that forces a child to introspection as the only way to really give vent to their emotions. If you put on too much pressure, something has to give somewhere. In the case of Wolfgang Priklopil his choice of a young girl who did not leave him feeling threatened, and his clear hostility to women exhibited in his conversations with workmates, does indicate that he may have had problems with his mother, or his utter dependence on her, his feelings of self-worth only activated by her doting attitude toward him on any given day. Equally it could simply have been that he was impotent.

The ability to enjoy sex and from this to build a happy relationship is one of the basic tenets of human existence. He may have felt cut off from life through impotency, and removed from society, and this may well have been the enormous pressure that he suffered.

I believe he must have suffered something that made him in turn want to inflict something on others.

What was it that Priklopil had experienced that made him feel the victim and want to escape from that by becoming the perpetrator? Look hard enough and all too often you will see the person beaten later becomes the beater.

Whatever the pressure Wolfgang Priklopil was under, it must have been enormous for him to have committed such a crime; his fantasy world must have been all consuming for him. He spent enormous amounts of time thinking and preparing what he was to do, and how to move from being the victim with no friends and no girlfriend to becoming the perpetrator, and turning the tables on the world. In his mind the fantasy world where he would snatch and mould the perfect woman merged with the real world, until he could no longer see the difference. The preparation he made in the cellar showed he was obsessed with this idea.

Ironically, though, what he saw as his salvation was always doomed to end in failure. From the moment he kidnapped Natascha he had made a choice to end his loneliness, and slowly over the years he would have learned to understand feelings and developed an intense relationship with this young girl who was totally dependent on his actions. From her he would have learned to become a better man, because he had to learn to think about her and not just about himself. It was as he allowed himself to care for her, and the healing process started, that his fate was sealed. Another life was not possible for him because of the way he had chosen to escape from his problems. What he had done gave him no chance of a return to normal life.

People are fascinated by this story because everyone can see it in black and white. They can empathise with Natascha, who was powerless to act, and can see themselves in the same situation and try to imagine how they might react. It is a normal human condition to put oneself in the place of another. But nobody would put themselves in the place of Priklopil; after all, he was a monster.

In the end his illness was cured: he had no fear of women any more, they no longer dominated. But at the same time the world he knew had ended: he knew he would never see again the woman who had brought him back into the real world. The image he had portrayed to neighbours had been ripped away and he would no longer have the thin veneer of popularity he had recently started to gain. His true self was revealed. The friendly Wolfgang, the new Wolfgang, could no longer live and he had no choice but to die.

Another opinion on Priklopil is supplied by Austria's most prominent court psychiatrist, Dr Reinhard Haller, famous for working on the cases of the mad bomber Franz Fuchs and the Nazi doctor Heinrich Gross: the decorated medical specialist who was revealed after the war to have been involved in the systematic murder of mentally retarded and handicapped children at a Viennese clinic.

In my opinion [said Haller] Priklopil had a very complex personality disorder, with very low self-esteem and strong fears of failure, most probably sex-related. He probably feared that he lacked manhood, and that is why he had chosen a child of that age. In doing that he wanted to grow out of his own infantilism and probably to overcome his infantile sexuality.

Being infantile as he was, he was not able to become a father in the normal way at the age of 34, so he had chosen to abduct a child and mould it according to his own wishes. Of course he also had a sadistic side and wanted to entirely dominate her, otherwise he would not have chosen a ten-year-old child.

There is no doubt he was bringing her up according to what he thought was right, while he underwent a certain process of maturing himself, so it could be said that they have grown together. But as she developed with time she became stronger and stronger and the balance of power in the relationship gradually shifted. At the end she probably became the one to make the decisions and she completed her transformation from a helpless child victim to a strong, grown-up woman who was in control. Once that happened, she was able to make a healthy decision and end the unhealthy relationship by running away.

One has to understand that the relationship between the two was very complex. At first she was confined physically, then psychologically, and at the end the strings became emotional. To her he was many things: a father, a brother, a friend and most probably a lover. The situation can to a certain extent be compared to that of fathers who abuse their own children: they also go shopping, out for walks, take holidays together and lead a seemingly normal life. The children are also not crying for help directly because they are tied with emotional strings that force them to keep silent.

Priklopil was very narcissistic, egocentric and very paranoid, which is what drove him to be meticulous in everything he did. He probably did not have any problem justifying his actions to himself and his victim. People like that are known to be able to rationalise their actions easily, they easily find their reasons in other people or sometimes blame the world for being unjust and so on.

His outward behaviour has been trained, that's why people always thought of him as 'nice', but not as emotionally hearty. He built up a big inferiority complex and at the same time established a great craving for relationship and family. What led him to become a kidnapper? I think it's because of genetic factors, but later on something must have gone wrong in his life. That could have been insulting comments when he had his first sexual contacts. Maybe it had been comments from his parents that he didn't like. He doubted himself, but at the same time there were sound relationships within his family. Apparently he was a good planner, and he was intelligent.

Natascha must have had something that appealed to him, so-called 'key stimuli'. That may have been her charisma, her body, the colour of her hair. I think that he chose a child who corresponded the most to his infantile nature. I can imagine that he wanted to lead her across to normality, quasi give her a new identity. He had wanted to mould and change her, until he may have thought that he could safely integrate her (and himself) into the outer world. He might have introduced her as 'my wife from Russia' or something like that, given time.

I don't think he would have killed her. But I can very well imagine some kind of 'advanced suicide', meaning that he would have dragged her into death together with himself when confronted with a hopeless and forlorn situation.

Georgine Malik, 62, who still lives just around the corner from Priklopil's house, declared herself to have been 'as friendly as it got' with the nobody whose name would become a byword for evil.

I knew him ever since he was a little boy [she said], and I also knew his mother well. They were good neighbours, very nice people, both of them. He was always working around the house and took care that his garden was tidy. He was a very tidy man, and he even helped the neighbours and cleared the snow off for them in winter. I often talked to his mum, she had a hard time after her husband Karl died of cancer in the eighties. She went to his grave every weekend. She was a bit unhappy about the fact that her son Wolfgang inherited most of her husband's assets. She also used to tell me how she was worried that Wolfgang would never marry, and that he was only interested in making lots of money and never dated any girls.

I once asked him directly if he ever planned to marry, because he was quite a good-looking man, and he replied that once he earned enough money he would move somewhere nice abroad and find a nice woman for himself there. That was his aim all the way, to make lots of money and then move abroad. But he never said where he would like to go to.

I remember he was very good with his hands, he was capable of building or fixing anything. He was very technical. He told me everything in his house was automatic, the blinds, the garage doors and all that. But perhaps gadgets took over from his contact with the real world. I never saw him with any friends, male or female, and I have certainly never heard of anyone seeing him in female company. Some people said that he could be homosexual, but I think that was just gossip. He was a nice person, very sweet.

In fact to his immediate neighbours the house had a nickname. When Priklopil eventually came to live there alone, he peppered the walls with security gadgets, including a high-tech video surveillance system, which Priklopil told neighbours were there to 'keep out burglars'. He told them never to pop round for a visit unannounced because he had 'built a number of surprises into my house and we don't want somebody innocent to get fried'. As a result, according to 66-year-old pensioners Josef and Leopoldine Jantschek who lived next door, the house was known locally as the 'Fort Knox of the Heinestrasse'. Josef Jantschek said:

I know it sounds awful now, but we had a good relationship with Wolfgang. How could we know something so terrible was going on? We used to stand at the fence with him for hours talking about God and the world. But Priklopil would act strangely sometimes, particularly when his mother came to visit. He would pace around the garden staring at the grass and looking in the bushes and checking every window, which he told us was just him 'cleaning up and making everything perfect.' It seems likely now he was checking that there was no evidence of his secret captive.

The mayor in Strasshof, Herbert Farthofer, was like the neighbours; he said he heard nothing to make him think there was a monster in the midst of the community, and added, 'He was not one of our problem residents. While we twice sent someone to change the water meter, they never noticed anything. Roland Paschinger, spokesman for the local authority, said, 'According to our records, we never noticed anything unusual.'

Hannah Arendt, the Jewish philosopher and historian who first coined the phrase 'the banality of evil' – about SS leader Adolf Eichmann when he was on trial in Jerusalem for his unparalleled crimes, crimes which included holding 21,000 Hungarian Jews as hostages in a concentration camp in Strasshof that was just a few minutes' walk from Heinestrasse – could so easily have applied it to Wolfgang Priklopil.

Most of the things he did, his individuality, certainly marked him out as a one-off – yet everything about him screamed sad, not bad. And nothing emitted a signal about the predator he was to become. He was a banal figure.

Because of this hiding-in-plain-sight demeanour, Priklopil was ultimately able to pull off that which all criminals dream about: the perfect crime.

Paschinger said Priklopil had once called the council in a 'furious rage' because the hedge around his house had been cut back too much, 'making it easier to see into the garden'. He went on: 'No one thought at the time – why? He was not someone who stood out, and you would never have imagined the truth. This sort of thing only happens in America, we thought. But we forgot a simple truth here – that evil people don't look evil.'

Another neighbour, Wilhelm Jaderka, said, 'We never noticed him. He never turned up in the local beer garden.' Yet another, Franz Zabel, offered up: 'This community is not a village any more. Many people are moving, many want nothing to do with anyone else. That is why people don't get noticed, or get noticed too late.'

At Rugierstrasse 30, where he used to live and where his mother still lives, until she was forced to go into hiding by the tumultuous events of August 2006, neighbour Charlotte Strack remembered Wolfgang as a timid creature who was afraid of her dogs.

> He had a terrible fear of my dogs Amor and Nando, even though everyone here in this block of flats knows that they would never harm anyone. If I happened to come across him when I had the dogs, he would press himself flat against the wall to get as far away from them as possible and turn white in the face. He would demand that I take the dogs away.
>
> When he moved away permanently to Strasshof he visited his mother once a week. Well, I think it was more pestered than visited. Through the ceiling I could hear how he screamed and ordered her about. He treated her like a slave.

Ernst Winter, the communications technician working at electronics giant Siemens who went through the company's training programme together with Priklopil between

1977 and 1981, also recalled the 'weirdness' that marked his friend out as different – his lack of interest in girls. 'He simply never, ever spoke about girls, which was unusual for us boys at the time. Weird. The only passion he had that I knew about was cars. He started racing in rallies at the age of seventeen. I think that was even before he got his driving licence.'

Winter also recalled: 'He was always quiet and liked to remain in the background. We all wanted to be the fastest to finish a job, but he would just take his time. He was very thorough and precise.'

During his time at Siemens, in 1981, Priklopil was absent for eight months' compulsory military service. Austrian data protection laws forbid the military from giving out any detailed information, but it is confirmed that he served at the Maria Theresien barracks in Vienna, a wartime SS barracks, using his skills in electronics as an intelligence communications specialist. He asked for assignment to a radio and reconnaissance battalion, but was never on manoeuvres or away for long periods. He was only confined to barracks for the first six weeks of his service, and neighbours remember that he came home most weekends, usually clutching a bag of washing for Waltraud to do for him. After the first six weeks he lived back at home for the remaining six and a half months of his compulsory service.

The relationship with his father was, by all accounts, an uneasy one. A man who liked sports and the clubby, manly chumminess of the local pub, Karl Priklopil found his son's solitary pursuits strange. Given the rumours that would later swirl around him when he lived alone with his mother, that he was either a latent or a practising homosexual, it is not hard to envisage the kind of arguments that might have ensued between a straight, conservative father and a son whom he somehow perceived as being deviant.

Deviant he certainly was, but not in the way that Karl suspected.

Franz Trnka, 49, who worked with Priklopil on the Austrian telephone network for the electronics company Kapsch in Vienna between 1983 and 1991 – Priklopil was made redundant from Siemens through downsizing – provided an unusual perspective. Unlike most of Priklopil's acquaintances, who depicted him as the shy, socially awkward loner, Trnka regarded him as a 'rude show-off', ill-equipped to face life's difficulties as they presented themselves. He also claimed that the kidnapper had inferiority complexes regarding women.

During the lunch break on Mondays the men would get together and talk about women, but Priklopil would always leave at that moment, so as not to have to hear anything on the subject. It was difficult to have a normal conversation about current affairs with him.

He had very limited interests: his BMW and its subwoofer stereo system, the electronic alarm systems he built in his parents' house and his model trains.

He could talk for hours to another colleague who also drove a BMW. To other people he made it clear that they were not worth anything to him, because they did not fit in with his schedule and interests. Whenever he could, he tried to humiliate someone in order to promote himself in some way.

He had an especially bad relationship with women. He perceived them as inferior and they were not worth anything to him. He would proudly tell us how he stopped women drivers from turning towards the exit on the motorway by blocking them with his car on purpose.

Experts think this quote goes to the heart of his compulsion to control. As one journalist wrote: 'The point was that they were female. They were driving – but he was in the driving seat.'

Trnka went on: 'He also wanted to show off all the time. He made sure everyone knew his family had money. But his father forced him to get a job – I think that was the only reason he was working at the time. He couldn't wait for his father to die, so he could inherit his money. He did not have a particularly good relationship with him.'

Karl Priklopil's father Oskar had been just as meticulous, in many respects, as his grandson. And it was his planning for a nuclear war that gave Wolfgang a ready-built room for his future 'dungeon'.

In 1950s Austria, a country outside NATO, families received grants if they chose to build atomic shelters in their homes. Perhaps because he had enough money, perhaps because he could not be bothered to wrestle with the tedious, energy-draining bureaucracy of the sort his country is infamous for, Oskar made no requests for cash from the state; nor did he apply for planning permission from the local authority when he set about constructing a doomsday sanctuary. Such independence from the state would be perfect for his grandson later on.

No permission, no records – it never existed. Ideal for what Priklopil Jnr would later do with the space.

The illicit shelter was later transformed into a utility room by his dad, and as a teenager Wolfgang helped out with the plastering and the drainage gulley. 'The bunker', as he would call it, would be used in turn as a storeroom, a workroom, a leisure room where his train set was stored and, ultimately, as a prison for a terrified child.

Elisabeth Brainin, another psychoanalyst – Wolfgang Priklopil's legacy to the world will be to keep the textbooks on the dark side of human nature churning out for decades to come – saw pictures of what the world has dubbed his dungeon shortly after Natascha was free. She commented: 'The whole things reminds me of extreme patriarchal societies, where ten- or eleven-year-olds get married by force to much older men. These men educate and finally make a woman out of them. It is possible that this man wanted to forge a woman exactly the shape he wanted her to be.'

It was in 1986 that Wolfgang's father Karl died of bowel cancer. Although workmates have spoken of the troubles that existed between father and son, the death seemed to affect him deeply. Experts say it is often the case for psychopaths that, when the object of their hatred or resentment is removed, they experience a kind of mourning. Wolfgang lived on in the Strasshof house alone after the death, but his mother chose to return to the council flat from where they had moved over a decade earlier: curiously, it had never been returned to the authorities for another family to live in. His mother began to play an even bigger role in his life.

He would return home from work at the Kapsch company, not to the Strasshof house, but to the flat, where his mother would prepare him Wiener schnitzels and potato salad, noodles with cream sauce or beef hotpot. He would later tell people that they sat together watching TV – quiz shows and old westerns were favourites – or leafing through photograph albums that chronicled the history of the Priklopil family. After a short while he moved in with her full time and only returned to Strasshof at weekends to check on the house.

There is a particular feature of the flat that is worth noting: it was very near to the school that would later be attended by a little girl called Natascha Kampusch.

Something changed in him in 1991, when, aged nearly thirty, he suddenly wanted to live alone. The shy teenager who did not like to be away from his family during his army service – who, in fact, had never lived alone except for brief periods during that time – chose to pack up and move back to No. 60 Heinestrasse. Here he would grow tomato plants in the dried-out family swimming pool, tune up the motors of his beloved cars and fine-tune the plans for the very, very special space beneath the garage floor.

While he fixated on one demonic plan, his mother remained the singular emotional prop in an otherwise lonely life, leaving the council flat most Fridays with bags of pre-cooked food labelled Monday to Friday which she had frozen so Wolfgang would 'eat properly' during the week. He also acquired two cats that he came to dote on. Christa Stefan, a lifelong friend of Waltraud, whose home in Strasshof faces Priklopil's, said: 'Waltraud came to stay with him here every weekend. She did all his cooking and housework, and either brought or made meals to be frozen for the entire week. She always said: "Wolfgang is my everything".'

Police psychologist Manfred Krampl believes that early on in the 1990s the obsession to kidnap a child was already crystallising in his mind:

Nobody could have anticipated at this stage, that Priklopil surreptitiously developed a rapidly growing need to have someone with whom he could communicate. Someone who is nearby all the time – a little girl he could possess. At first Priklopil ran through this scenario – or his vision of this scenario – in his mind. Then he 'decorated' it in daydreams. By kidnapping the little girl Priklopil would create some kind of parallel world, his very own insular realm, undetected and unknown by everyone else. A realm in which he rules everything.

And I think it all came down to a single thing – that he had a severe deficit in the ability to form normal human relationships.

Even when plotting to bring to life the kidnap fantasy, Priklopil still indulged in the cruelties he enjoyed from childhood. In 1992 a retired policeman, Franz Hafergut, out walking in the neighbourhood with a weather eye on property and people, reported him to his still-serving colleagues when he saw him eating cake and shooting birds, this time not with the DIY gun he assembled at school but with a .22 calibre air pistol he had bought for £60. He received a warning not to do it again. Otherwise, apart from one or two motoring offences, he was never in trouble with the law again.

With his neighbours it was a different story. Many remember him as odd at best, often downright rude, even deeply strange. Peter Drkosch, 68, who lived nearby, had known him since he was a boy. He and his wife Hedi owned an allotment with a small summer-house that they stayed in often just opposite 60 Heinestrasse. The proximity irritated and upset Priklopil, as Drkosch recalled:

Before we did the allotment up he regarded the land as his 'rocky field' where he used to wash his car. Therefore he didn't like our allotment at all. He would have preferred to live in isolation and tranquillity.

He could also be a real bellyacher. At lunchtimes he always started mowing his lawn when it was the 'quiet time'. In Austria you are supposed to respect people's privacy between midday and three, and not do things like mowing lawns or trimming hedges. But not him. He always started mowing with a big lawn tractor. He only did this in order to antagonise other people. He was a bit bossy and, when working, a nitpicker. Until now, everyone thought he just had a lot of fads. For example, when somebody parked their car badly, he immediately reported it to the police.

The police would duly come along, unaware of what the complainant had 'parked' beneath his garage. Herr Drkosch went on:

There were constantly arguments, as Priklopil used to park his car on the small road behind his house in a way that prevented other neighbours from passing by and accessing their property. Just before he died he hosed down the whole road and the water was almost three centimetres deep. I first thought a water conduit had broken, but then I saw a hose coming out of Priklopil's garden. Then he came and alleged the local authority had assigned him to take care of this place and water it.

Another neighbour has a much more disturbing memory of him. Stefan Freiberger said: 'My eight-year-old daughter, and another neighbour's child of the same age, were riding their bikes in the nearby forest because there are a lot of raspberries and blackberries. Suddenly he came and took off his clothes. He was completely naked. The children naturally were afraid and returned home immediately. My wife tells me to this day that we should have called the police.'

Priklopil's seemingly easy access to cash, his fancy cars and apparent lack of regular work hours made neighbours believe that he either had a private income or had had a windfall. 'I always wondered where he got all the money from that he needed for building,' said near neighbour Rosemarie Helfert. 'It was always rumoured that he'd won the lottery.'

'In my eyes, he didn't work at anything,' said Peter Drkosch.

> He would leave by car at seven in the morning and would return two hours later. In the afternoon, he would leave again. During the last three weeks, he left three times a week at three in the morning – my wife always woke up because of that. When he came back with his Mercedes van, he stopped at the gate, opened it, drove his van on to the property and immediately locked the gate again. When he would leave an hour later, he would do the same. He always locked the gate.
>
> In June this year, I saw him working on the roof, telling a woman who was standing on the ground that she should hand him the drill and his tools. It was a young voice, and I thought, finally he has a girlfriend. He would certainly be the right age for that. Once my wife was in the garden, and she heard that voice too. He would speak differently to his mother; the young voice he always addressed with a commanding tone.

Local postman Hermann Fallenbüchl, who delivered the mail in the Heinestrasse, said: 'I never spoke to him and I saw him maybe once a month, no more. He was very polite, greeted me in a friendly way and waved from his car. Only once did I see an old woman – it must have been his mother.'

'Priklopil was a phantom in the town,' said Fallen-büchl.

In the early 1990s Priklopil forged a business partnership with the one individual who seemed to be a true friend to him. Ernst Holzapfel, who was quizzed by police after Natascha escaped, was cleared of any involvement in her kidnapping and detention, but if Priklopil had chosen to reveal his secret to anyone it might have been him. He would even come to meet Natascha a month before her breakout and, like the neighbours who never suspected, thought she was merely a friend.

Holzapfel was a pal from the Siemens days and invited 'Wolfi', as he called him, to join him in a business venture, the Resan construction and renovation company. The pair started out renovating old properties and then branched out into the entertainment business, staging birthday and wedding parties at a gaudily decorated warehouse on a Viennese industrial estate. The pair made money and 'Wolfi' was able to indulge himself in his cars – 'bombing up and down country lanes', as another former Siemens workmate said. He once received a speeding ticket for £50, and on another occasion was involved in a minor accident in which no one was hurt.

People around the Strasshof house began to refer to Priklopil as a 'Bachener' – a colloquial, derogatory term for homosexual – although Holzapfel claims he never saw this side of his friend and business partner.

* * *

The 'realm' referred to by police psychologist Manfred Kram – the realm in which he was going to rule everything – would be the erstwhile shelter beneath his garage. He meticulously set about making this into an undetectable, soundproofed, windowless void – the only way for fresh air to reach it would be through a ventilation system controlled from above by him. He bought the materials necessary for the conversion from everyday DIY stores, always paying cash.

He bought a desk for the intended victim to use. He installed a small sink and toilet, plumbed into the mains, and used insulating material of the kind favoured by music recording engineers to make the chamber soundproof. After Natascha finally escaped, police lifted floorboards inside his house to reveal stairs leading down to a maze of doors and passages. Underground, detectives found a metal cupboard, behind which was a tunnel barely big enough for a person to squeeze through. At the end of the tunnel was a makeshift concrete door leading to yet another passage and finally the room where Natascha was held. Her world measured barely more than 5 square metres, with a bed on a raised platform and its ladder used to hang clothes.

This was the end station of Wolfgang Prikopil's life: a hole in the ground, 3.5m by 1.8m by 1.5m, to which childhood isolation, an all-forgiving motherly love, a few fragile friendships and an increasingly powerful compulsion had somehow led him. His work training and innate skill with his hands allowed him to build it without too much effort. This much we know – what remains as murky as his own hideous motives are the circumstances which led him one day to choose Natascha Kampusch as the resident of this subterranean pit.

Apart from his council flat, the Strasshof house with its prepared dungeon and the home of Natascha, there is a fourth location that is central to the complicated existence of Wolfgang Priklopil. This is Christine's Schnellimbiss, a lowly truck-stop cum fast-food joint in a dreary outlying district of Vienna – far removed from the period grace of the old imperial capital's still imposing buildings – where Priklopil downed the occasional non-alcoholic drink. It is central, and not a little chilling, because it is a place that Natascha's parents used to go to and, according to her father in interviews with the authors, Natascha herself. Ludwig Koch would never walk from his home to the pub near his house: for 20 years he would drive across town to Christine's.

Christine's is at the corner of Obachgasse and Rautenweg, which is about five minutes' walk from the Rennbahnweg estate and on the route between Priklopil's council flat in the Rugierstrasse and his house in Strasshof. It lies in the most down-at-heel part of Vienna's northern industrial zone, close to the city limits, among construction companies and discount DIY markets and just across the road from an enormous garbage processing facility, a pyramid-like metal building that towers over the grim area.

The bar's clientele consists mostly of workers from the nearby companies and drinkers from the neighbourhood, many of them from the Rennbahnweg estate. The bar itself is a run-down wooden shed with six bench-tables. With a mental measuring tape the casual observer can calculate it to be about eight times the size of Priklopil's underground cell.

The owner, Christine Palfrader, is a bulky woman in her early fifties who is fed up with the glare of publicity, the TV cameras that come barging through the door, the Klieg lights and the swarms of irrepressible reporters. But she remembered Wolfgang Priklopil.

It is a miracle, a miracle that she is alive and well. But we all know there is more to that story. God only knows what has really been happening. As for Priklopil, he was sometimes here several times a week, but we did not know his name until we saw him on TV. He was a quiet man, always very friendly and polite with everyone. He used to stand at the same place at the counter each time. I cannot remember precisely what he ate or drank, but I think it was usually a sausage and it was never alcohol – maybe an apple juice mixed with sparkling water, something like that. I don't remember when he first started coming here. He was not someone you would notice or talk about.

He only talked to two other technicians, some stuff about their job. They both admired him and said he knew a lot about his work and was a really clever man. We all had the impression he was educated and smart, and he always dressed smartly too.

He was handsome, good-looking, but somehow

unnoticeable. He just did not stick out. You could say he was invisible. The only thing people noticed him for was his flashy car. He had this big sporty BMW that he would park in front of the bar. The engine used to make a lot of noise, so people would turn and look.

I last saw him in July 2006 before closing down for three weeks for the August holidays.

Also a regular at the bar is Natascha's father Ludwig, known here by his nickname 'Luki'. He stops here after knocking off the night shift at the bakery where he is now employed, to eat breakfast and drink a beer or wine spritzer at seven in the morning in his back-to-front, nocturnal life. The question has still not been answered: did he meet 'Wolfi' without knowing who he was? Did he engage him in conversation one day, ask him about the weather?

Did he even buy him a glass of apple juice without knowing that, some seven to ten minutes' drive away, depending on the traffic, his little girl was captive in this man's specially constructed gaol? Christine cannot recall ever seeing the two men together. But there is yet a further twist in this bizarre Bermuda triangle of intertwining acquaintances and happenstance meetings.

A former 'good friend' of Ludwig's, who was also a boyfriend of Natascha's mother, Brigitta Sirny, has also been named as knowing Priklopil. Ronnie Husek owns a haulage business in the industrial estate around the corner from the snack bar. 'I know Husek a bit. Frau Sirny knows him very well,' says Herr Koch. 'He used to be a friend of mine, but no longer.' That is because Herr Husek began an affair with Frau Sirny when she and Ludwig were still together, claim neighbours.

In this poor part of Vienna, witnesses have reported seeing Herr Husek with Priklopil at a grocer's shop that Frau Sirny used to run: Husek bringing him around so that the technically gifted loner could fix a faulty fuse box.

Among the witnesses is the strictly anti-Sirny Anneliese Glaser, who had a clear memory of the visit: 'And I am sure she knew Priklopil, the kidnapper. I remember him very well, he came to the shop with this Husek, Ronnie Husek, and was fixing the fuse box outside. It was in September 1997, just before she lost the shop. Frau Sirny then came too and she talked to them both. I know that Frau Sirny knew Husek, and it would make sense that he called a friend of his to fix the fuse box, and this friend was obviously Priklopil.'

Frau Glaser says she told detectives on the case of her suspicions, but claims they were apathetic, to say the least, about her allegations. 'I believe this story needs to be investigated. There are many things that need to be clarified. Natascha did not tell the story about the night before, and this bit is missing in reports. I would like to meet her again, Natascha, to talk to her.'

Husek is also said to know Wolfgang's business buddy Holzapfel. So far he has refused to speak about any friendship. In fact, he has not spoken since he gave a press conference after Natascha reappeared, in which he said he met her while she was in captivity but didn't know who she was.

Can it really all be a coincidence – the perpetrator drinking in the same pub as the victim's father, with the man who became the lover of the victim's mother and who knew Priklopil's business partner? But there is more. Natascha Kampusch was there with her father. In an interview with the authors, Herr Koch, his emotions spent along with his money, could not be certain of having seen the kidnapper at the bar, but revealed that he had been there with Natascha:

When I first saw his pictures on TV he did seem familiar to me. It's possible that I had seen him at Christine's or elsewhere, but I can't remember. I certainly knew his car from the neighbourhood, I saw it several times. It's quite noticeable, it's not a model you see every day.

I've been going to Christine's for at least 20 years, I forget exactly how long. If I went there at a time when I was looking after Natascha then I would always have taken her with me because I always had her with me, I never left her alone. Yes, I can say she has been in there with me, that's true, but don't ask me for dates.

I know the owner really well, I've been going there since it opened. I just don't recall ever meeting Wolfgang Priklopil there but I had seen him somewhere.

Kidnapper, captor, friends, parents, all in the same bar, all simply thrown together? Did Priklopil, seeing her there, somehow tell himself he would be saving her from what he judged a wretched life if he took her? Did Natascha exchange a glance with him there, a friendly smile across the smoky saloon? Did she meet any of those regulars or hear them come to the house when she was a captive?

However it came about, the plan that had been growing in Wolfgang Priklopil's mind for many years was about to come to fruition on 2 March 1998. For the next 3,096 days, Natascha Kampusch would vanish from the face of the earth.

3

The Abduction of Natascha

'Hello Ernst, Wolfgang. I won't be in tomorrow. Got something up.' With these few words Wolfgang Priklopil launched the abduction of Natascha Kampusch. He called his partner the evening before and then set about preparing. He checked that everything was ready in the special room. He laid out underpants and towels, arranged the childrens' books that he had bought in shops far, far from his neighbourhood. And he programmed the security and ventilation systems one more time, ensuring that the compressed air pump that would keep his trophy alive was working, along with the plethora of intruder alarms and video cameras vital to keep his secret safe.

Shortly after 6 a.m. on Monday 2 March, as radio newscasters were informing him that it was the birthday of *perestroika* architect Mikhail Gorbachev, that the last will of the late Princess Diana had been published, and, closer to home, that a walker had discovered a 5-kilo anti-tank shell from the Second World War in a Viennese suburb, Priklopil drank his coffee, set the numerous alarms on his house and went out into the wet, dark morning. He started his white Mercedes van and drove off for the rendezvous with the little girl who, on this day, would cross over the line from his special dream to his special possession. Nothing could stop him now: nothing could save Natascha now.

Both were drawn inexorably to the time and the place where worlds would meld, change and shatter.

At flat 18 in block 38 on the Rennbahnweg estate Frau Sirny was up extraordinarily early, reading through complex paperwork regarding the bankruptcy of two grocery shops she once owned. She recalled making several cups of coffee as she ploughed through the weighty documents, going to the bathroom and calling Natascha to get up at around 6.40 a.m. to be on her way to school. Natascha was due to have a special lesson in German and was supposed to be there early. Frau Sirny had quickly prepared her daughter's clothes and a row developed that ended when she slapped her on the ear. In fact, the argument was a continuation of a squabble between them the evening before. On the previous Friday her father had collected her for one of their trips to Hungary. He was supposed to drop her off back at home no later than 6.00 p.m. on the Sunday but, as usual, to the constant irritation of his former partner, he failed to be on time. It was 7.45 p.m on Sunday 1 March when he deposited her outside the tower block. One of the last things she did before kissing her 'papi' goodbye was to reach into the glove compartment of his car for her passport in the left-hand pocket of her jacket. She then trudged into the gloom of block 38 and hoped the lifts were working.

She let herself in but found she was home alone. On her bedroom door there was a note from her mother: 'Gone to the cinema. Back later. Mutti. X.' This was a common occurrence: Natascha was something of a latch-key kid whose mother did not run her life around her. She was used to arriving home to an empty flat.

Natsacha changed into a tracksuit and went to a neighbour who knew her well. Frau Glaser, who would later make claims that began to warp the public perception of Natascha as an accidental victim, once worked for Frau Sirny. She has assumed, in the media whirlpool that continues to swirl in Vienna, the mantle of older sister, the woman who was ready to step in and help 'poor Natascha' when her mother wasn't there. Frau Glaser, who lived one floor below Natascha and her mother, claimed that on this night, after welcoming the child inside, she sent her back upstairs to leave a note for her mother in case she came home early and panicked if Natascha wasn't home.

Ludwig Koch brought Natascha back from a weekend trip to Hungary sometime between 7 and 7.30 p.m., a bit later than it was agreed with the mother, who was by then already gone. I remember that day so clearly, as if it happened yesterday. I will never forget it.

Natascha came to my flat and told me her mother was not at home, so we tried to call her on the mobile, but it was off. I then told her to leave a message for Frau Sirny to say that she was at my place. Natascha was in a good mood, she told us about how she had had a great time in Hungary and about all the things they did there with her dad, Herr Koch. We had a nice conversation, small talk – she was such a bright kid and very nice to talk to.

We than had some dinner, but it was hard to persuade her to eat anything because she had already eaten some hours earlier. Afterwards we watched *Columbo* on TV – she liked that series. It was fun watching it with her, she made funny remarks, much like an adult.

But then her mother came, sometime around 9.45 p.m., and started shouting at her right from the door, she did not even say hi to us. She told her that it was wrong to come to my place and that she was supposed to stay at home, alone.

Then she sat down and the two of us, Frau Sirny and I, had Baileys to drink. But she kept shouting at her daughter, insulting her and all. I felt very embarrassed and told her to calm down.

Frau Sirny than told Natascha to go upstairs to their flat, change her bed sheets and go to sleep. Natascha was wetting her bed, and the mother was telling everyone about that. She reproached her because of it in front of me, and I could see that the girl was very ashamed of it.

After Natascha went home, Frau Sirny stayed with me and had more drinks and went on about how Natascha was becoming more and more cheeky with every new trip to Hungary. But that was not true, she was not cheeky at all, and she also loved the trips to Hungary – she would always return happy and positive from there.

Anyway, it was such a shame that the evening had to end like that. Natascha had been very happy, and she'd told me that her mother had cleared out the baby room in the flat and she believed she was finally going to get around to getting her a writing table, which was something that seemed very important to her.

Natascha was, indeed, just hours away from getting such a table – but it was in a hermetically sealed room in Wolfgang Priklopil's strange home, not her own.

She went to bed sullen, feeling unloved and put-upon. And the combination of a bad night's sleep and the dreary prospect of an early start at school for a test in the extra German class she'd been attending, meant she was late in getting up. Some 20 days later, in virtually the only interview she has ever given about the family life surrounding Natascha, Frau Sirny admitted to the Viennese paper *Kronen Zeitung* that there were words the next day about her tardiness. It got more heated, in the way these things do, and her mother lashed out, giving her a firm slap around the face. But as soon as it was delivered, it was regretted. Frau Sirny told the paper: 'On the morning she disappeared, she stayed in bed for 45 minutes before getting up. She is generally bad at getting up. Then she could not find her glasses. And then she was cheeky. So I gave her a smack in the mouth. But I don't persecute myself because of it. One must set limits with children. But yes, she was obviously emotionally hurt.'

Natascha dressed in silence, stopping only at the door of the flat as her mother turned to give her a hug, saying, 'You must never set off for school upset or angry with me, because we may never see each other again.'

One lost childhood later Natascha would reveal in her TV interview: 'Yup, the second of March 1998. A bad day. On the evening before, I had a fight with my mother because my father brought me home too late and didn't accompany me to the apartment door. "God knows what could have happened to you," she said to me, "someone could have grabbed you" – and then the next day, while in her care, that really happened. "Never leave the house after an argument without saying goodbye," my mother always used to say.

'Exactly. And I thought, "I don't agree with my mother right now," and to spite her I slammed the door. Because nothing was going to happen to me anyway. That's pretty heavy when you are kidnapped just half an hour later and you are cowering in the back of a van.'

Less than a mile away, Priklopil the predator waited. He parked his van in the Melangasse near to her school gates. White van man, inconspicuous as ever throughout an unremarkable life, waiting for the moment that he had prepared for over the years. The collector, come to collect that which he knew would fulfil him the way no jigsaw puzzle or electronic circuit breaker ever had. He sat, silent and alone in his van, tuned into the local Vienna news radio which, 24 hours later, would be featuring as its lead item the news of a missing girl. The windows of the van were misted from his breath on the inside; the windscreen was running with rivulets of melting ice and snow on the outside. People walking to work paid no heed to a solitary driver waiting for a passenger. Priklopil had counted on his anonymity helping him on this, the most important day in his life, and he was not let down. Herr Nobody. Perfect.

The slap from her mother was still stinging her cheeks as she came close to the end of her cold, weary 15-minute trudge with her heavy satchel of schoolbooks, while luckier school pals drove past in their parents' warm cars. Splashing through the dirty brown sludge that the previous day had been crisp, white snow, it was not only Natascha's school bag that was heavy but also her heart – the youngster was deeply unhappy both at home and at school.

As she dwelt on her problems, the young girl noticed a man staring at her from a vehicle in front of her just 500 metres from her school. But she was wrapped up in her thoughts and suppressed her feelings of uneasiness at the stranger and continued towards him, pulling her thick red ski jacket around her and bowing her head against the icy wind.

It was a decision that was going to cost her over eight years of her life. And it wasn't until her time in hell was over that she could tell the world what she thought and felt in those last moments of being a schoolgirl before she was captured to satisfy Priklopil's demented urges.

'I saw the man and thought there was something strange about him. I knew I should have gone over to the other side of the street, but for some reason I didn't,' said Natascha. She admitted she wasn't really concentrating because of an argument with her mum, who was angry because Natascha had slept through her alarm and didn't get to sleep until late the night before. Her mother had argued on the phone with her father after he had dropped Natascha off late after the Hungarian weekend break. 'And I was tired,' she recalled.

Natascha said her mum was also angry because she refused to wear her glasses, which she thought made her look ugly, and that had provoked the slap across the face. She was walking towards calamity, splashing in the slush, her face down, her thoughts concentrated. Then she saw his Mercedes van and something gripped her . . . not exactly terror, just a feeling of unease. There were only a few paces to go now and she slowed down a little, but was still walking towards the van. She would mentally flagellate herself for her decision later. Why didn't I cross the road? Why didn't I walk with some other kids or an adult? Why didn't I listen to the voice in my head telling me that something was wrong here? But time was running out. Drawn inexorably towards the innocent-looking white van, unaware of the evil that sat waiting for her in it.

Did the unhappiness in her life shroud her judgement? Was the sting of that slap – in itself nothing major but a totem of the stresses and antagonism that lived with her at the flat – blocking out reason? 'What if?' is a question that can be asked about so many things in life. All Natascha knows is that if she had crossed the road she would not have been living in a pit.

But maybe she would have. As her captor would later tell her: if not that day, then another. She was, after all, the chosen one. The real threat the van-man posed, however, only dawned on Natascha when he grabbed her and pulled her into his vehicle. 'The man climbed out of the van and was suddenly beside me. He grabbed my arm and threw me inside before shutting the doors and speeding off. He shouted at me and said I should be still and quiet or there would be trouble,' she said of the nightmare journey that was just the start of her ordeal.

'Are you going to rape me?' Natascha's mother, speaking to a journalist in Vienna years later, after her daughter was freed, claimed these were the first words that Natascha spoke to Priklopil. Does this show an awareness of sex and sexual things outside the normal remit of a ten-year-old girl? Or is it merely another marker of her intelligence?

Discussing the actual kidnapping, she said he growled at her that nothing would happen to her if she remained still and did not move. 'And do as I say and you won't get hurt,' he added for good measure. A few minutes later her told her it was a kidnapping and that if her parents paid a ransom she could go home 'that day or the next'.

Natascha's thoughts went into overdrive. Fear and confusion jostled for pole position in her young mind. She said she had no fear initially – but then admits that she thought he might kill her. 'I had heard of children who were raped and then quickly buried in the woods somewhere. And I thought I could put my last few hours or minutes or whatever to good use, and at least try to do something. To escape, or to talk him out of it or something. I told him that it wouldn't work and that going against the law never prospers. And that the police would soon get him and so on.' She told herself that if she could remember details, of his face, his van, his house when they got there, they would aid police when the time came to capture him. Later she would say: 'At that point I was sure the police would get him and it would all have a good ending.'

It would not have a 'good ending' – at least not for a very, very long time.

But before Natascha was driven to the Strasshof house, Priklopil took her somewhere else. In her interview with the *Kronen Zeitung* shortly after regaining her freedom many years later, she said enigmatically: 'We didn't drive directly home. I don't want to falsify history, but I will say no more.'

This statement is pregnant with implications. Where did she go? Was it to meet someone – an accomplice perhaps? To buy something? To sightsee? This was a kidnap, wasn't it? Isn't urgency and haste of the essence in such a situation? Is Natascha trying to protect someone here, other than the memory of the kidnapper who she ultimately felt sorry for? The riddle remains unanswered, both by her and the police.

It goes to the heart of the Natascha–Priklopil relationship. There are secrets to preserve somewhere in this saga.

Eventually she was driven to the Strasshof home while Vienna stirred in the half-light of the wintry morning, dragged from the car, pushed with some force into the pit and left in total, utter darkness. She was snatched at around 7.20 a.m. and arrived in the dungeon some time later that morning, the ever meticulous Priklopil having been careful not to trigger the speed cameras on Federal Highway 8 that led to Strasshof and his sinister, hand-built lair.

Natascha's prison was a masterpiece in technical planning. Priklopil documented every stage of the construction process with pictures later seized by police. The prison is accessible through a staircase in the floor of his garage, the entry hidden under a white cupboard. The flight of stairs leads down to a metal door and behind that a 150-kilo door made from iron and concrete. This door can only be opened and closed from the outside with concealed threaded rods. This leads into an anteroom where a door decorated with pink hearts – Priklopil's concession to femininity and youth – leads to Natascha's actual prison. The room is absolutely sound-proof. On one side there is a loft bed, on the other a hanging cabinet, a desk, a chest of drawers, a basin and a toilet. Electricity for lights, radio, TV and the fan can be switched on and off from the outside and with a time switch respectively. Natascha was provided with fresh air through a complex electronic ventilating system. She described her initial impressions:

The first time I didn't really see it [the dungeon] because it was pitch black. There wasn't a light on there or anything. He only fetched one after some minutes, I don't know, maybe half an hour. I was very distraught and very cross and angry that I hadn't crossed the street or gone with my mum to school. That was really awful. And the powerlessness. Crying because I was powerless to do anything. I was really angry and didn't know what to do. It was awful – the feeling of being powerless, of not being able to do anything. That was the worst. I could hardly stand the noise of the ventilator at the beginning, it got on my nerves so much. It was horrible. Later on, I just jumped out of my skin at any noise. I felt claustrophobic. There were no windows and no doors. I couldn't see anything. I didn't even know if anyone

could hear me outside. He said my parents did not care
for me and were not looking for me. And later he told
me they were in prison.'

Wolfgang had got what he wished for.

Yet the instincts Natascha had learned at home were
already kicking in. She had been left on her own by her
family many times – nothing strange or frightening in
that. She had been subjected to roller-coaster emotions
that left her bewildered, with no one but herself to rely
on. Once again, like a soldier who has been trained to
withstand isolation in a prisoner-of-war camp, she could
compartmentalise: I am alive – check. I am unharmed –
check. I am dry, I am intact, I am not being tortured –
check, check, check.

The amazing thing is that she was able to marshal
this calm, this almost tranquil state, at an age when
she was still wetting her bed, still liked to sleep with
the light on and still, despite their troubled relationship was deeply dependent on her mother. That filial
love would not break despite all the minutes, hours,
days, weeks, months and years that were to follow on
from the first stunning moments of this horrendous
captivity.

When the light eventually went on she took stock of
her sealed world, saw the things that Priklopil had laid
out for her with his indefatigable neatness and love for
order. Natascha had arrived in the clothes she stood up
in, and with her satchel that had a few pens and pencils
inside ready for her German grammar test. She would

never know, at least not for years, that the police would later be looking in her room in the flat to make sure they were with her, checking on the truth of the statement that she had gone to school to take a German test.

She saw he had bought what she described as 'baby cutlery, with big fat teddy bears' on them – carefully chosen instruments designed not to harm their toddler users – or him. The cup was plastic, not glass. There were no scissors. This indicates that Wolfgang Priklopil, however certain he was of the righteousness of his cause, was capable of realising that maybe the object of his desires may not have been as overjoyed as he was with this new life hidden beneath concrete, steel, planking and soundproofed tiles. He didn't want his captive to have tools to hand that she might use on him.

Natascha's mother, who later recalled having waved goodbye to her daughter from the window of the apartment, left for work at a company called Meals on Wheels, at 7.30 a.m. She was late, because she had to stop to pump air into a faulty tyre on her car, and arrived at 8.45. When she finished work at midday she went to her tax adviser's office, where she made a phone call to a friend. On the way home, by coincidence, she found herself driving alongside Natascha's father, and so slowly that she was able to wind down the window to ask if he knew where Natascha's passport was. 'I couldn't find it last night in her bag,' she said, but admitted she hadn't looked in her jacket.

Some time later she arrived home, where she met her lover. When her daughter was still not home by 4.50 p.m. she became nervous and called her son-in-law, who she knew had collected both his children. She thought they might know where Natascha was. A call to class-mates made it clear that Natascha had not been in school that day. As a result Frau Sirny went to the police. Ludwig Koch was only made aware at 8 p.m. when he was called on his mobile phone and told that his daughter had vanished.

When it emerged later that evening that Natascha was missing, after not turning up either at school or at her after-school kindergarten where she spent the afternoons while her mother was at work, police initially believed she had run away from home. As a result they failed to launch a proper search for her until over 48 hours later. It was just the start of an eight-and-a-half-year investiga-tion that is now being seriously questioned, the police having missed or failed to act on vital leads that could have revealed the child's whereabouts.

Dr Hannes Scherz, who was leading the police inves-tigation at the time, said hours after she vanished: 'At the moment we are not sure if Natascha Kampusch is the victim of a crime or has simply run away from home. Natascha lives with her mother but also has a good relationship with her father, where she spends every other weekend. It is possible she ran away to find her dad.' This despite the fact that there were three unsolved murders of females from a few years earlier in the area that were still raw in the public conscience. Alexandra

Schriefl, 20, Christine Beranek, 11, and Nicole Stau, 8, were raped and murdered. Eventually a man was sentenced to life imprisonment in 2001 after DNA linking him to the murder of Stau was recovered.

For the police, the Natascha case was a riddle they never solved: one they never came close to solving.

There were few victories scored by Natascha in those first hours of captivity, but her captor had not escaped entirely unscathed. The day following her seizure he was treated at the nearby Korneuburg Hospital for an injury that almost severed his middle finger.

The chief physician of the hospital, Dr Wolfgang Hintringer, said: 'He claimed that he got his finger jammed in a safe door. The finger was almost severed, but it healed very well following the intervention.' It is accepted that Priklopil, who had no safe in his home, almost certainly caught his finger in the heavy steel door he had installed to keep Natascha secure. It weighed 150 kilos and his finger bore all the signs of having been trapped in something that exerted tremendous pressure.

Dr Hintringer also indicated that Priklopil visited the hospital once more about a year after the kidnapping. He said: 'He fell in some hole at a construction site and had several bruises.'

As great as the coming nightmare was to be for Natascha, it was to become one she would manage, to compartmentalise, to get through each day gaining concessions from her zookeeper. For her parents it was a nightmare without end, particularly for her mother who had to endure the guilt which that final, temper-fuelled slap had injected into her conscience. And because she knew the police were trying hard at times to swerve the inquiry in her direction, to link her with the abduction.

Frau Sirny claimed that for over eight years she prayed every day that her daughter would be returned to her, and that she knew in her heart that she was alive:

> I always said that one day she would come back. Maybe she would be a different Natascha, but she would come back. Her disappearance ruled my life ever since she was taken from me at the age of ten.
>
> Every day I prayed that she was OK and told her to hang on in there and hoped that one day she would come home. Each year I would celebrate her birthday by baking her favourite chocolate cake. It was never eaten, but somehow remembering the little things about her and what she liked helped me to get through.

Frau Sirny says she tried everything to find her daughter, including hiring clairvoyants, some of whom assured her she was still alive. Her father Ludwig, too, forfeited all life's trivialities and pursuits after she was taken. He cursed himself for not having tried harder when he split with her mother to gain custody of Natascha. Like her mother, he was reduced to scouring the streets of the ancient capital in a desperate search for her.

Frau Sirny said, 'In the first few weeks I trawled the streets of Vienna looking for her. I would sit in parks all day in the hope that she would turn up. Then I started to travel to other Austrian towns and cities and hang out in places where there were lots of children, especially kids who had run away from home or were skipping school, but there was no sign of her.'

When the police told her there was little else they could do and were scaling down the investigation into Natascha's disappearance, Brigitta Sirny sought help from psychics.

'I didn't know what else to do, and so I went to a clairvoyant to ask if she could help me. She told me that Natascha was alive. She said that she was being held north of Vienna in a cellar in a house, but the police refused to act on the information, saying the psychic was probably just a hoax.'

Also painful, even in the aftermath of reunion, was the knowledge that she had driven to Strasshof one day for work and had actually travelled right past the house. 'I can't believe I even drove past it one day when I had a presentation in Strasshof,' she said, her head bowed, her eyes filling up with tears.

Even as the days, months and years passed, she said it never got any easier for her:

What really got on my nerves was everyone giving me bits of advice, especially when they said things like 'Life goes on'. For me it was like being in a time warp. Life around me went on, but in my head it stopped on the day Natascha vanished.

At times I even wished they would find Natascha's body. At least then I could have strived towards some kind of closure and had a grave where I could mourn my beautiful daughter. But instead I continued as if she would walk through the door at any minute. I saved any letters she got and kept her things as she had left them. In my bathroom I made room for her Barbie shampoo and her Pocahontas soap. One day I discovered that Natascha's clothes had been eaten by moths and I almost collapsed with sadness.

At Natascha's school her loss hit hard and deep. Many schoolfriends recalled the fateful day she vanished from their lives. Michael Ulm, who was in the same class as Natascha – 4C – fell ill with worry because she had gone. 'She was my friend,' he said. 'I want the person who took her away to bring her back.' Schoolchildren pleaded with teachers to be allowed to form search parties to scour the streets and wasteland nearby, but the idea was soon scotched for fear of more unsupervised children going missing.

Mothers who took their children to school were the lucky ones: most parents were too busy working to ferry their offspring to the gates and to pick them up again. Gabriele Boehm, 38, who started escorting her son to school after Natascha vanished, said: 'Most mothers work around here. You can only hope every day that things will turn out OK, but there are no guarantees – we know that now, don't we?'

Liane Pichler, 45, was upset that the authorities hadn't seen fit to inform the mothers that another school in the area had posted a warning about a sex criminal they believed was stalking children in the area. Whether or not the suspect was Wolfgang Priklopil will now never be known.

Newspapers at the time printed the messages of hope and love that they hoped would touch a nerve in a stony-hearted man:

YVONNE: Hopefully, you will come back to us soon.
KATHARINA: I was her best friend and she told me everything.
JENNIFER: She told me that there was lots and lots of rowing in the house and that she was often sucked into them. She didn't like that.
MARCEL: She was inventive, funny, strong, quiet – sometimes – and cheeky. And she could sometimes scratch and bite.

The children were allowed, after a time, to take her books home with them to keep as totems of the pal they lost. For a long while her seat was left empty in school, a reminder that they never stopped thinking of her. But as the years passed and her pals grew up, it was occupied by other pupils as the memory of her, inevitably, faded.

'We pray each evening for Natascha,' said her form teacher Susanne Broneder, who added that a planned excursion for the pupils to see *Amy and the Wild Geese* had to be cancelled because her chums were too upset at her vanishing.

The headmaster back then, Guenter Willner, said the only way to carry on was to believe in a happy ending.

He thought that if his pupils believed Natascha had gone for ever, many of them would have been unable to cope.

Numerous children came forward to say they had seen her on the morning she went missing. Bettina Hoffmann, 12, said she saw her 'not more than 100 metres from the school gates. She was heading in the direction of the school.' But Bettina had not seen what happened next.

Twenty-one children, her school classmates, went off to a local church for a special prayer service. Their prayers went unanswered for over eight long years.

Well-wishers left flowers at the door of Natascha's flat, while others who had lost children, through illness, accident or murder, wrote letters of condolence to Ludwig and Brigitta. None of them could know she was alive, well, and beginning her slow metamorphosis from victim to victor in a cellar three metres below ground just a few short miles from the old bedroom which her mother visited every day to draw strength from her spirit.

In 2002 Frau Sirny admitted in an interview with the Austrian magazine *Woman* that she knew, for certain people, she was a suspect. The interview went thus:

The Sonderkommision (SOKO) has recently reopened the Natascha case. That Frau Sirny, Natascha's mother, is one of the prime suspects now, does not shock her. That she was informed about these new investigations through Teletext, however, did surprise Frau Sirny, as she tells us in the WOMAN interview:

Woman: How were you informed about the recent renewed investigation by the police into the disappearance of your daughter?

Frau Sirny: I was sitting in my car, when my cell phone rang. My sister-in-law informed me that she had just read the news on Teletext.

Woman: Have the investigators established contact with you yet?

Frau Sirny: No, and that is precisely what makes me so angry. They did not think it was worth the effort to inform me about this. I called at the Bundeskriminalamt several times . . .

Woman: What did they tell you?

Frau Sirny: Nothing. Because none of the gentlemen was able to talk to me. I asked them to call me back, but am still waiting!

Woman: What do you feel about this?

Frau Sirny: It's not acceptable, that they just leave me standing in the rain, that they have me run after them.

Woman: There are plans to search for your daughter at a lake near Vienna. What do you think about that?

Frau Sirny: If they want to dig, let them dig. If they think they are going to find something there . . .

Woman: But shouldn't you be relieved that everything is checked again? Relieved to possibly find out what really happened to Natascha?

Frau Sirny: Yes, actually I should. Maybe they over-looked something back then.

Woman: Before they find the offender, everyone who was close to the victim is under suspicion from the

investigators. Therefore also you, as Natascha's
mother. How do you handle this?
Frau Sirny: What am I supposed to do, if they suspect
me again? I have to accept that. I will definitely co-
operate.
Woman: The owner of the lake is a friend of yours.
What does he say about these planned diggings?
Frau Sirny: He said they should just go ahead and
dig . . .
Woman: Have you ever had any ideas about what
might have happened?
Frau Sirny: No. Never!

Police later had to admit that Frau Sirny had been
dropped as a suspect in the case.

Time passed, the seasons blending into one. Ludwig Koch lost his businesses one by one as he
ploughed money and time into trying to find his
daughter, prowling the streets late at night, scrutinising the waifs outside the city's West Station to see if
she was among them, looking at the young hookers
in the red-light district, asking anyone and everyone
to look at the photo of Natascha he carried around
with him.

'Have you seen this little girl?' he would ask. 'Have
you seen her with anyone?' But the strays, the junkies, the
hookers, the flotsam and jetsam of urban life, answered
with mute shakes of the head.

Frau Sirny, too, coped with her own private hell – first
the animosity of her husband, then of people like Anne-

liese Glaser. Placing faith in clairvoyants gave a little comfort and hope, but only a little. Nothing could make up for the loss of her flesh and blood.

The agonies were piled on whenever headlines surfaced in another country of a child killer – and the worst pain came in 2004 when 62-year-old Michel Fourniret, the 'Beast of France', hit the headlines as the mass murderer of at least nine women and girls. He took some of his victims in a van similar to the one that a witness had told police she had seen someone dragging Natascha into. Frau Sirny said in an anguished interview at the time:

About three weeks ago, late one evening, when I saw a report about the arrest of this man, and found out that he frequently used a white van when he was looking for victims, I immediately thought about Natascha. And I began to pray: 'Please not, please not, my kid cannot be one of his victims . . .'

I only know: there are so many things that would match up. The thing about the white van is just one of them. But in the meantime I have also found out how this killer approached his victims: that he pretended to be sick and needed help. And Natascha was always helpful: she would only have come near a stranger if she felt that her help was really needed. Then she would have surely approached him. And I don't want to think any further: the thought that my child became victim of this beast is just awful.

Asked in the same interview if she still clung to the hope that Natascha was alive, she said: 'I will never lose that hope, until I know, one hundred per cent, that Natascha is dead. And in my dreams it happens every now and then, that my little girl suddenly stands at the door and says: "Mommy, now I'm back." And waking back up is so awful, because I'm back in reality, and there is the terrible uncertainty . . .'

If she could have known how her daughter was conducting herself in those first few hours she would have had nothing but pride in her. Natascha would later say: 'In principle, I knew within the first couple of hours of my abduction that he was lacking something. That he had a deficit.'

She would go on to say that he had a 'labile personality' in contrast to what she judged a 'healthy social environment around me – maybe not a particularly happy, but a loving family. Both my parents had assured me that they loved me. He didn't have that. In a certain way he lacked self-assurance. And something else – security. He didn't have that.'

A labile personality. A complex word describing a complex complaint, learned by a little girl who taught herself such things in her cellar world.

Her freedom was to the psychoanalyst's profession what war is to armaments industries, with theories about him, her, her family and relationships piling up like wrecks at a stockcar rally. But she was closest of all to Priklopil in a hothouse environment unencumbered by other social contact. Perhaps her take on him is one that has more value than any of those 'experts' who would swarm around her after 23 August 2006.

A labile personality is described as manifesting itself in people who are chaotic, whose relationships are stormy, short-lived and unstable. Those who suffer from Borderline Personality Disorder often display a labile – wildly fluctuating – sense of self-worth and self-image and affect emotions they do not really feel.

Sam Vankin, an authority on such types and author of *Malignant Self Love – Narcissism Revisited*, said:

The main dynamic in the Borderline Personality Disorder is abandonment anxiety. Like co-dependents, Borderlines attempt to pre-empt or prevent abandonment (both real and imagined) by their nearest and dearest. They cling frantically and counterproductively to their partners, mates, spouses, friends, children, or even neighbours. This fierce attachment is coupled with idealisation and then swift and merciless devaluation of the borderline's target.

Borderlines shift dizzyingly between dysphoria (sadness or depression) and euphoria, manic self-confidence and paralysing anxiety, irritability and indifference. This is reminiscent of the mood swings of Bipolar Disorder patients. But Borderlines are much angrier and more violent. They usually get into physical fights, throw temper tantrums, and have frightening rage attacks.

Curiously, most borderlines are women, but not all, and a woman, Wolfgang's mother, was the single biggest influence on his life. Weak, violent, dependent, sometimes self-hating . . . Natascha spotted the weak spots in her kidnapper's armour from the outset.

This would be priceless ammunition in the war of wills against Wolfgang Priklopil.

4

Life in Hell

It is unimaginable, but we must try to imagine it. We must try to place ourselves in Natascha Kampusch's skin if we are to understand what she went through in her man-made grotto. The asthmatic wheeze of a ventilator pumping in tepid air, the light which went on early every morning and faded out each evening, the utter silence: no birdsong, no chit-chat of neighbours, no watching the vapour trails of planes high in a blue sky or hearing the friendly rustle of leaves blowing in mini tornadoes in a garden. When it was dark down there, at night, or if Priklopil had turned the light off in some temper fit, it was akin to complete sensory deprivation. It is the kind of mind-training undergone by élite soldiers to enable them to survive torture in captivity and to keep their sanity when lost in deserts or jungles. It is not meant for little ten-year-old girls thinking about cats and dolls and homework left undone. The experience compresses time: although the experience is unpleasant, if the captive has no access to timekeeping – as Natascha did not have for the first few months – time, paradoxically, seems shorter than normal time. In one test in the 1980s a subject who spent 58 days underground to gauge the effects on both psyche and body thought he had been under for just 33. But Natascha could not have known that when she awoke after her first night; nor could it have offered much comfort if she had.

Whatever the shortcomings in her upbringing, she had been schooled by her parents, like all children everywhere, to beware the bogeyman, not to accept lifts from strangers, not to talk with them outside school gates, nor take sweets from anyone offering them. Kindly policemen, either too fat or too old to pound the beat any longer, had come to her school to hammer the same message home. Now, on 3 March 1998, as the light in her cell came on at 7 a.m., she realised all the nightmares had come at once. It is testament to an incredible will allied to a keen intelligence that she rallied, marshalled the forces of resolve and said to herself: this will not beat me. I will survive.

If she emerged as a remarkable young woman, it was because she went in there as a remarkable young girl.

Later she would be asked if she cursed the fate that put her, rather than anyone else, three metres below the ground. She replied: 'No! Straight after the kidnapping I asked myself what I did wrong. I asked myself if I had done anything to the Lord God. I was seriously in despair. I had claustrophobic feelings from that tiny room and it was really harrowing. And I had no idea what was going to happen to me; whether they would kill me, what they would do with me. At the beginning I thought there were many offenders.'

But there was only one. At the time of writing the police have just finished their lengthy investigation of the crime scene. They used sniffer dogs and, after pumping in artificial fog in a bid to find other possible hiding-places for other potential victims, could find no other secret chambers or hidden, deceased girls. They dragged numerous bags of earth away from the site and continue to pore over the ancient, Commodore computer he used (which wasn't connected to the Internet) to see if its relatively primitive memory holds any secrets of his plan or of what he might have subjected Natascha to over the years. Or if he had an accomplice at any time for his diabolical scheme.

Yet while detectives believe that he may have had contacts with other perverts, they are certain he acted alone in the kidnap and only had one victim – Natascha. Heat-seeking sensors and rods pushed deep into the earth around the property have turned up no unmarked graves.

'Gebieter,' he said to her during their first meeting after she was taken to the clandestine jail. 'That is what I want you to call me.' 'Gebieter' is German for master, and it shows that from then on Wolfgang Priklopil intended to shed the persona of the seven-stone weakling who always got sand kicked in his face. He was to be in charge in a way that he had never been in charge of his life. But Natascha never once bowed to his wish.

Criminal psychologist Thomas Mueller claims he was 'a high-grade sadistic perpetrator, who wanted complete control over his prisoner. He wanted the power of life and death over her.' Despite the books of fairy stories he bought, the videos he would later let her watch, the clothes he chose, the toiletries, cutlery and food, he was staking his claim to superiority.

This was the moment he had waited for, had rehearsed in his mind a million times for the sexual frisson it gave him. Master! Ruler of a strange world with a population of two. It was a time to cherish and, while he always celebrated birthdays and Christmas with Natascha, in his mind the best anniversary of all would remain that of the day he acted, finally acted, and brought her into his world. In fact, made her his world.

Aside from nearly severing his finger in the steel trap door when he had first locked her inside the dungeon, this was his first mistake. Natascha was a wilful girl in freedom: if anything, in captivity, she became even more so. In spite of his size and the situation he had forced Natascha into – his complete control over her movements, her total severance from her family – if he had dreamed of a pliable beauty for his secret room he could not have been more wrong. In devoting himself to his Pygmalion-style task, to make her love him, he had embarked on the road to his own destruction. She was not the obedient wallflower of his sick dreams, as he would soon learn.

Naturally, there was terror instilled into her, particularly in those first hours and days. She fought the horrors that jostled for space in her mind, stricken with anxiety that she would run out of water or air or food. She feared that he might become involved in a road accident and not be able to come and rescue her; the precise theme of a story in a *Pan Book of Horror Stories* from the 1970s in which a hapless, cellar-bound female kidnap victim is reduced to a rat-eating, half-mad skeleton after her captor ends up in hospital for six months after a road crash.

'When he was going out of the house I would always wonder: how long would he stay there – hours? The whole day? The thought that something could happen to him . . . an accident, a heart attack. Then I would never, ever get out. How long would the ventilator last? Longer than I would?'

Someone else in her situation might have said to themselves: 'If it makes him feel good to be called master, then why not?' But not Natascha. She steadfastly refused to bend to his wishes.

Subservient she may have been: sugar, she would tell police later, always gets you more than vinegar, no matter what the situation. But beg? Not Natascha Kampusch's style.

Paying lip-service to his grandiose ideal of himself was a far cry from bending her will to him. That she refused to do from day one. That is why she would later say that everything that went on between them was voluntary. That is why she remains convinced he never broke her. 'I was always the stronger one,' she said. 'I think he had a very bad guilty conscience, but massively tried to repress it and deny it. That shows in itself that he felt guilty.'

So they embarked together on this unnatural journey, one which would consume the rest of her childhood, her puberty and some of her young adult life before it ended. They forged the accommodation which fulfilled his fantasy and allowed Natascha her small victories which, ultimately, added up to a great many.

For the first six months he never let her out of her prison. She had books – the fairy stories, mostly, even though Natascha had long outgrown those before she fell into his clutches – but no TV or radio during that period. She ate, performed her bodily functions, washed, slept, cried, dreamed and grew stronger in her isolation. She saw him regularly but there have been few details from her of what they discussed. It is known that they read together and that she began to look forward to his company: when you have nothing and no one to talk to, say the experts, then 'Stockholming' is bound to come into effect.

'Stockholming', or Stockholm syndrome, is a psychological response sometimes seen in an abducted hostage, in which the hostage exhibits loyalty to the hostage-taker, in spite of the danger in which the hostage has been placed. Stockholm syndrome is also sometimes discussed in reference to other situations with similar tensions, such as battered person syndrome, child abuse cases, and bride kidnapping.

The syndrome is named after the Norrmalmstorg robbery of Kreditbanken at NorrmalFrautorg, Stockholm, Sweden in which the bank robbers held bank employees hostage from 23 to 28 August 1973. In this case, the victims became emotionally attached to their victimisers, and even defended their captors after they were freed from their six-day ordeal. The term was coined by the criminologist and psychiatrist Nils Bejerot, who assisted the police during the robbery, and referred to the syndrome in a news broadcast.

Yet what Natascha underwent, and the period she underwent it for, required a new term for a new phenomenon, and after it was all over it was called 'Vienna syndrome'. Stockholm syndrome became a redundant phrase for a young woman who would, in many senses, start dictating the pattern of life at No. 60 Heinestrasse.

In her curious 'Letter to the world', released after the maelstrom of publicity that engulfed her when she was finally free, she told of how that daily life developed:

This was carefully regulated. Mostly it started with a joint breakfast – he was anyway not working most of the time. There was housework, reading, television, talking, cooking. That's all there was, year in and year out, and always tied in with the fear of being lonely.

He was not my master. I was just as strong as him, but he would, symbolically speaking, sometimes be my support and sometimes be the person who kicked me. But with me he had picked the wrong person, and we both knew that.

Indeed, evidence that she was the 'wrong person' came within the first few weeks of captivity. Priklopil had installed a bell in her chamber that she was to use to call him if she wanted anything. She used it so much and so often that, in a fit of frustration, he simply ripped the thing out. Another point to Natascha.

After that first dark night, in which she hardly slept at all, a kind of routine developed.

> I always got up very early, the lights would turn on automatically at 7 a.m. There was a certain order and structure, but there was no spring, summer, autumn or winter. Not like for the other children, who went to school, and went on holidays and went into the arms of their mothers. At night the light would not go off so precisely, but sooner or later it would get dark.

She explained that her captor regularly brought her books of her choice: 'At the beginning I wanted the children's classics like Karl May, *Robinson Crusoe* and *Uncle Tom's Cabin*. I was reading and reading.' The Karl May books she particularly liked were about the Old West and the immense bond of friendship between a cowboy, Old Shatterhand, and Winnetou, an Indian brave. Like Natascha, Karl May had never travelled to America when he wrote the books. Like him, she would dream of the vast open spaces, trying to visualise them from her captivity.

Unlikely compadres, Old Shatterhand and Winnetou. A bit like Natascha and Priklopil.

* * *

For the first six months she was not allowed upstairs. She had to take showers in her dungeon, with a mineral water bottle with some holes in it. This was replaced by a hose with a kind of shower head attached to it. She was later allowed to take showers or baths upstairs, every week or every two weeks. She would be let out under the intense scrutiny of her captor. He would check security monitors, ensure that no one was approaching the house, and keep the blinds drawn and the shades down before leading her from the dungeon to the bathroom. He had installed special locks on the bathroom window, and there was no lock on the bathroom door, so he could burst in if he felt she was up to anything other than her ablutions.

As soon as she was given permission to move around the house, Priklopil started bringing her video tapes; for example, episodes from *Star Trek*, the 1980s television series *Magnum* and recorded Austrian TV programmes. Police later said he was 'very economical' with his tapes. He had hundreds and hundreds of them, and every inch of usable tape was recorded upon, even if it was snippets of news items or advertisements after the main programme he had wanted to record was finished.

At some point he installed a TV and radio in the dungeon. 'So I developed myself more and more,' said Natascha. 'Because I was reading so much, I thought to myself, I could also start to write books, novels. I started writing in different notebooks, it wasn't only the diary.'

Were these books about escape, about love, about

imprisonment, a sort of pre-pubescent *Papillon*? Natascha has kept them as secret from the world as she did from Priklopil.

While she was committing her thoughts and dreams to paper, she said Priklopil respected her privacy. She recalled that he never came into her 'room' – she referred to it variously after her escape as her room or her dungeon – without knocking.

The 'master' was reduced to acting in the manner of a servant in a remarkably short time. It was evident, too, that harming Natascha was not on the agenda. If he wanted her to love him he was prepared to do anything, and that included performing to an agenda rapidly being dictated by her.

She went on: 'My diary and everything I wrote belonged only to myself. He could never take a peek into it. He never got mixed up in my private things. But he intervened in a humiliating way when it came to random daily things, like the way I was supposed to wash my toothbrush and things like that. But my writings belonged to me alone. And he also never entered my room just like that, unannounced.'

A pattern was emerging which would put Natascha, in a bizarre, but strong position. She was coping better than many adults would. Major-General Gerhard Lang, the spokesman for Austrian police on the Natascha case, reported how he had himself locked up in the dungeon for five minutes in order to try and understand how she felt during her captivity:

I have seen a lot in my time, but this is another dimension. It is impressive how complicated it is to access, how well hidden it is and how small the actual space is, when one is inside.

She was locked up in there for over six months before she was allowed to go out. I was there for less than five minutes and I could hardly take it. The silence, the hopelessness and the despair of the feeling of being cut off from the whole world outside. It must have been horrible.

Imagine how a child aged ten would feel, locked up like that. She told us she was hitting on the walls with plastic bottles and screaming for help. But it took over six months before he allowed her to go up, and that was only to take a bath or use the toilet.

Professor Max Friedrich, Natascha's chief psychiatric adviser, said: 'She was subject to isolation torture. That is the worst kind of torture of them all, when one is completely cut off from the world.'

Police believe that Priklopil exerted extreme self-discipline upon himself during the early days and weeks of her captivity. He had acquired that which had tormented him, and now the question was how to 'enjoy' it.

Did he rape her? She has not commented on any sexual liaison, and police and the experts surrounding her have divided opinions.

The first policewoman she had contact with after regaining her freedom spoke of 'sexual abuse'.

Natascha refuses to answer any questions regarding

'intimacy' – a stance which in itself indicates that intimacy there was. In one of her enigmatic replies to police interrogators in an interview later printed by Austria's *News Magazine*, she said: 'Wolfi was no sex beast and neither was I. We had a tender relationship.'

But the question of the physical side of this relationship, forged by circumstance and developed by her own forceful character, will not go away. Natascha, who surrounded herself with lawyers immediately after her breakout, threatens to sue newspapers worldwide who call her a 'sex slave', even though she refuses to say what happened between them. The Austrian media have quoted several police sources saying it was 'inevitable' that she was abused, although she refuses to admit or deny that any sexual relationship took place.

If she had sexual contact with him before she was sixteen, then he was guilty of breaking the laws of Austria and most other western nations. If any occurred after she was sixteen, and it was consensual, then Priklopil could only have been held to account for taking her in the first place. The way he chose to end his life, just when she began hers again, stopped a great deal of midnight oil from burning in the corridors of the Austrian justice ministry.

This reticence on Natascha's part muddies the water of the whole saga and her choice of words makes it hard for the world to understand how 'tenderness' could be applied to a man who had snatched her. Just how this tenderness was expressed, in any physical form, is a secret still locked within Natascha. She became a young woman with an incredible capacity to both understand and empathise with her captor: after she was free she even asked the media to stop writing about him, because she felt the details would upset his elderly mother.

Tender – perhaps sometimes. Other times he could, and easily would, show the hard, calculating side that had led him to take her without compassion in the first place. 'He told me that he was continuously calling my parents,' she recalled. 'They could have me back if they were ready to pay him 10 million schillings [approximately 500,000 pounds]. He showed me a piece of paper, on which he had written the telephone numbers of my mum and my dad. But he told me that neither was ever picking up. Because I was obviously not so important to them.'

Her kidnapper started using terms such as 'We are sitting in a boat' – a German phrase implying partnership and isolation from the rest – as well as saying things like, 'You and me are the only ones who matter' and 'We belong together for ever'. They occasionally watched TV news reports about the hunt for Natascha. Sometimes she had the eerie experience of watching police officers hunting for her body in places far from the little suburban house of horrors.

According to Natascha, over the weeks and months Priklopil tried to break her down with a mixture of violence and care. She said that she soon realised that when she was 'good' she would be rewarded with new books, clothes and sweets – so she tried to be 'good'. And Priklopil set about trying to create, in his own image, the beauty he hoped she would grow into.

He travelled to stores far from his home so as not to arouse suspicion. He bought her make-up sets and a wide range of cosmetics, tubs of Nivea face cream, and small make-up cases to keep it all in. He also brought her teen magazines so she could read how to apply lip gloss and dye her hair correctly. He had occasionally mentioned to acquaintances how hard it was to find a beautiful woman who understood him, but that he was sure that one day he would find his 'beautiful dream woman'.

Natascha said that the incredible sense of isolation she as a ten-year-old felt in her dungeon actually led her to look forward to Priklopil's visits.

At the beginning I didn't know what was worse: when he was with me or when I was alone. I only came to an arrangement with Priklopil because I was afraid of being lonely. When I was good with him, he spent a lot of time with me; when not, then I had to be alone in my room. If I couldn't have gone into the house now and then, where I could move, I don't know, maybe I would have gone crazy.

Priklopil had never had a girlfriend in his life, let alone a child. Intuitively, however, he seemed to know how to become a father figure to Natascha, how to exploit her vulnerability in order to underwrite and support his immorality.

She explained how the kidnapper slowly earned her trust by becoming this authority figure, teaching her geography and history and reading girls' books and adventure stories with her. She added that 'he brought me books to read and I asked him totally normal children's questions' about foreign countries and animals, which he reportedly always answered.

Her kidnapper also read her fairy stories about princesses who were rescued by noble knights as a metaphor for their life together. He claimed to be the only one who really cared about her. It was a not-so-subtle attempt at brainwashing, at manipulating a mind still forming and susceptible to adult influences. Yet it almost seems as if she let him have just as much influence as she wanted to give. She wanted to remain in control. By seeing with the crystal clarity of a child's eye early on how flawed he was, she was able to manipulate him later to the point where they lived a seemingly normal life.

When, after the 'long time' of isolation, Priklopil started taking Natascha out of her prison, and upstairs into his house, she repaid the privilege of being let out by doing what he asked, which was household chores, cooking, cleaning. They would eat together and sometimes she was allowed to watch a film with him. He would tell her stories about his childhood and show her photos of his mother. Police have said the Priklopil clan was a family addicted to the camera: dozens of albums containing hundreds of snapshots of Wolfgang, his father, grandparents, mother, cousins, aunts and family acquaintances were found at his house.

These used to be the centrepiece of a ritual he always

played out with Waltraud whenever she came to stay, looking back at times past instead of to future happiness. Now it was Natascha's turn to share them, and in knowing him, hoped Priklopil, she would come to love him.

Apart from the photograph-gazing sessions, which often went on for hours, he would try other, clumsier tactics in a bid to divorce her thoughts from her family. He would sometimes bring out a newspaper report about the kidnapping and its aftermath, saying: 'Look, they are still writing about us,' and then following it up by saying her parents had given up on her. Translation: I am all you have.

But that was untrue: in the surreal playing-house existence that life became at No. 60 Heinestrasse, Natascha always had so much more. She had parents she loved, cats, a life. It was he who always had so much more to lose than her, and she knew it:

I wasn't actually lonely. In my heart I had my family. And I always had happy memories. I thought about all the things I was missing out on. My first boyfriend, everything. I tried, for example, to be better than all the people on the outside, or at least be the same as them. Especially when it came to schooling. I had the feeling that I was missing out on something big. That I lacked something. And I always wanted to change that. That's why I tried to gather knowledge and to educate myself. And to teach myself skills. For example, I taught myself how to knit.

Some long-term prisoners use the time of their incarceration to hone their bodies: Natascha chose to train her mind. It was an extraordinary feat, say the experts, to on the one hand be living in fear of someone who has taken you away from your family, and on the other be able to compartmentalise that trauma so that learning and knowledge can be absorbed on a daily basis and with a high degree of competency.

Some 1,400 days into this bizarre life, Priklopil bestowed upon her what he obviously thought was a great honour – she could call him by the nickname that his mother and only his closest friend and business associate Ernst Holzapfel knew him by. As she put it: 'After around four years he said I could call him Wolfi, because during that time we had gotten to know each other well.'

She said: 'At some point we started to have a very normal life together. We talked a lot and watched TV.'

To continue his hold over Natascha as she entered her teens, Priklopil told her horror stories of the real world and backed them up with newspaper reports about alcoholics and drug addicts. He told her: 'Look, I've been protecting you from all these terrible things.' Yet at the same time he concocted James Bond-esque fantasies about the booby traps in the house that would be triggered to kill her if she ever tried to run away.

Natascha feared, given the fragile state of his mind, that he was permanently heavily armed, and that if she made even the tiniest of noises, he would trigger explosions that would kill them both. Neighbours reported that he once used the expression 'grilled to the bone' to describe the fate of any intruders foolish enough to breach his formidable DIY security system. It is also possible, of course, that he was bluffing.

Seen in hindsight, many aspects of life in Strasshof have the elements of a slightly dreary sitcom: her as maid cum servant cum cleaner and him as the breadwinner relaxing over his stuffed beef rolls and potato dumplings after a day at work, the pair of them probably bickering over whether to watch a comedy or a war film on telly that evening. But the undercurrent was always one of menace. He had taken her by force and she remained there under the constant threat of harm. The secret – Natascha – had to remain just that and for ever. Blinds and shutters were drawn on the sunniest of days, a sensor and video camera alerted Priklopil if anyone was about to come up the path. Then Natascha would be bundled back into her hiding-place. That was the one constant that never varied during the whole of their time together; he never lost sight of the fact that what he had done, and continued to do, was wrong, and that discovery would mean the end of everything.

It was particularly gruelling for Natascha when Frau Priklopil came, as she did most weekends, bearing food and groceries to 'keep my Wolfi's strength up'. Back to the cellar she went, hearing only the faintest of sounds above but smelling the cakes Priklopil's mother baked, the aromas wafting through the ventilation system pumping the life-giving air into her cell. These were the delicacies she would be allowed to eat after his mother had gone. Priklopil risked visits down to her at night, after his mother had gone to bed, but never during the day.

Psychiatrist Dr Haller, who has been following 'this most fascinating' of cases, said that the young woman did not just see her kidnapper in a negative way but indicated that there could have been a love relationship between the two. He said that the letter she wrote to the media years later revealed that Natascha was indeed not locked up in her cellar room all the time, but lived what resembles a normal life with her captor. He added: 'Priklopil was not only the dominant and cruel kidnapper, but also a father, a friend and possibly a lover. The diversity of their relationship, which is proving so difficult to express, is probably a reason why she wants her private sphere protected at all costs.'

This 'diversity' is a complex one and goes far beyond Stockholming. One British newspaper went so far as to say that Natascha became the 'hostage from hell'. A crude label, intended to imply a swift reversal of roles.

Despite the times he had to stuff her back in her room, who was really in charge here? She had gained enough trust from him to sit and watch movies with him, read books with him, cook and clean and perform all those housewifely duties conservative Austrian men expect from their Frauen [wives]. And she remained mentally alert and strong, teaching herself high German from a radio he installed in her dungeon, learning about far-away places on nature documentaries. Priklopil, on the other hand, just remained what he always was: a deviant creature who could only measure his self-worth by having her around.

After she freed herself the complexity of her character was assessed by Professor Ernst Berger, who was put in charge of co-ordinating Natascha's socio-psychiatric team. He said: 'The public have a one-dimensional image of Fraulein Kampusch and I realise that the complexity of a person is difficult to understand for most people. But like others, she has also got two and more sides to her personality. On the one hand she is immensely strong and very much in control of what is happening around her, but on the other she is quite weak and very vulnerable.'

Everything she is now, he said, is as a result of her time in that windowless void of her dungeon and playing housemaid for Priklopil. He went on:

Some aspects of her personality are very infantile. For example, she told me she wanted to live in an apartment with a security guard at the gate and a security camera system.

It is a bit unusual for a kidnapping victim to be keen on appearing in the media after her ordeal, but you have to understand that the media were her only contact with the outside world.

During the time of her captivity she only received input from Herr Priklopil and from the media he allowed her access to. So in a way, those were her two eyes that she saw the outside world with. It is therefore no wonder that she has a special relationship with the media.

Of course, there is a certain narcissistic component in

her desire to appear in public, but that is probably part of a defence mechanism. As we know from Anna Freud, if one individual defence mechanism becomes too independent and gets out of control, it could lead to psychological anomalies.

So far we have not had any evidence that Fraulein Kampusch suffered actual physical violence, she did not speak about beatings and she had no traces of it on her body. There were some blue spots on her legs, but they were not a result of violence.

However, she did tell us about three forms of torture she was subjected to: hunger, light and air. The kidnapper had control over her food intake, he controlled the light in her living space, and also the ventilation, the amount of air in her room.

These forms of torture also have a somatic aspect, for an example the hunger torture, and in that sense one could say that she did suffer physical torture. Fraulein Kampusch, however, lived in some kind of union with Herr Priklopil. We know about their occasional trips to the shops, we also know about the one-day skiing holiday. She also helped him renovate and decorate an apartment he wanted to let. She painted the walls and helped him with his work. They also went shopping for building materials together and picked some of the items. At home, in his house, she would cook and do the housework. In a way she had the duties of a housewife. He told her he would kill anyone who would try to help her escape, and this was blocking her thoughts about escape.

Despite the apparent normality of the grotesquely abnormal situation, Natascha insists that she first formulated plans for escaping when she was just twelve: 'By the age of twelve, or around that age, I started dreaming about breaking out of my prison . . . But I could not risk anything. He suffered badly from paranoia and was chronically mistrustful. A failed escape attempt would have meant that I would never be able to leave my dungeon. I had to gradually win his confidence.

'At the age of twelve I basically promised myself that I would escape. I told myself, my "I", that I would escape, and never abandon any thoughts about escaping.'

Asked how she coped with loneliness, she said: 'I had no loneliness. I had hope and believed in a future . . . I thought about my family during the whole time. For them the situation was even worse than for me. They believed I was dead. But I knew they were alive and fading away because of worries about me. At this time I was happy to be able to use my childhood memories as a way to freedom.'

Of her captivity, she said: 'Sometimes I dreamt of chopping his head off, if I only had an axe. Obviously I would then reject all that because I can't look at blood and I would never want to kill a person. I continuously looked for logistical approaches to a solution. First the escape, and then whatever was to come next. Was I simply to run into the streets of Strasshof, screaming, going to the neighbours?' Asked if Priklopil had threatened her, Kampusch said: 'Yes, but before, I didn't have any fear. I am freedom-loving and for me death was the final freedom, the release from him. I knew that he would kill himself.'

As this strange life continued, the outside world passed her by. In February 2000, in Austria, a right-wing party led by bogeyman politician Joerg Haider entered a power-sharing government. On the streets of downtown Vienna, a few short miles away, protestors clashed with police, and the world's opprobrium rained down on the country. In November of the same year 155 skiers lost their lives on the funicular railway fire at the ski resort of Kaprun. Both events requiring massive resources of police manpower: both events that eclipsed a long-lost little girl who hardened detectives and child charity workers were now convinced was dead.

One year previously, Natascha was still in her media blackout phase, so she never heard or saw the 1999 broadcasts on radio and TV shows by 61-year-old popular clairvoyant Rosalinde Haller, who said she could feel 'the energy of Natascha'. She went on: 'Already back then I suggested that she was in the north-east of Vienna, past the pond for bathing in Hirschstetten. I saw the kidnapper as a slim man, around 40 years old,' says Haller, who had already offered her help at the mining disaster in Lassing 1999, and who 'saw' the tsunamis that devastated parts of the world on Boxing Day 2004 in her book published five years earlier. Natascha *was* north of Vienna, but such vagueness triggered no new police momentum to try to find her.

At some point in 2000 Priklopil allowed Natascha limited access to papers, TV and radio. Life on the outside came to be viewed through the prism of what Priklopil wanted her to see and hear. As well as being her gaoler, he acted as censor. But Natascha was hardly the kind of person interested in frivolity. She liked listening to serious news programmes on her radio and watching nature documentaries. She recalled: 'For the first two years I didn't see the news. I was just scared. Then I got a radio, and I could hear the Austrian news again. It was quite emotional really.

'Sometimes I would get a weekly newspaper. He read it, then I would read it. He had control of everything I did. He checked I hadn't left any messages on the newspaper or anything like that.' Checked so that when he threw it away, no garbage worker might find a clue as to what he kept in his cellar.

Although Hollywood films fascinated her, she found articles and programmes about the private lives of the stars prurient and of no concern to anyone but themselves: a yardstick she would apply to the media and herself when the long confinement finally ended.

In the only TV interview she gave shortly after her breakout Natascha gave another clue to the slowly changing nature of the captor-captive relationship at No. 60 Heinestrasse. She told how she insisted that Priklopil shower her with Easter eggs, Christmas and birthday presents, saying:

> I forced him to celebrate those days with me. Other children or young people can buy things for themselves: I obviously could not. And he was obviously

thinking that he would give me at least some kind of compensation.

Every once in a while he even in some way suggested how I could escape, as if he wanted it. I kept telling myself to escape, to do something. I told him, 'It's not the right thing what you are doing. The police are out looking for me.' I always felt like a poor chicken in a hen house. You saw how small my cell was. It was a place to despair.

The desperate need to control, to dominate, married to his innate animal instinct that she would bolt if he let her outside, meant that the touchy-feely life of watching *Star Trek* together, eating meals that she had learned to cook from books he bought for her, washing, tidying, cleaning, sewing, preparing shopping lists for the food she would cook that evening, ended each day with a return to the dungeon and the slamming shut of the impenetrable steel door.

One side-effect of this housebound existence was to reduce the effectiveness of Natascha's immune system. Because she was not exposed to the everyday germs and viruses carried around by people, this would hit her hard when she was finally free. She also felt she suffered some kind of heart problems during her captivity, as she later said:

I also had problems with my heart one day; it was not all that great. I had all sorts of symptoms such as tachycardia, cardiac flutter, heart rhythm disturbances.

Meaning, it would suddenly stop and then go on pumping again. I got dizzy, at one point I could not see anything and everything disappeared. It was probably caused by the constant lack of nutrition.

But how was I supposed to have a doctor in my dungeon? I know it was all a result of the fact that I got too little food to eat.

When asked to elaborate on her heart problems, she said: 'I didn't receive any treatment; he only kept annoying me and giving me grief and had me carrying bins full of earth.'

The controlling of her by controlling her food is an interesting aspect of her confinement and one that seems to contradict the otherwise cosy aspects of their time together.

During my captivity I was starved very often. And I know about everything that comes with it: circulatory problems, concentration difficulties. You are only able to have the most primitive thoughts. You cannot focus on anything. Every sound, every scratch is exhausting and painful. I can well imagine that these people must go through unbelievable suffering.

We always make out that we are so clever, but if we didn't get all the food we do, then we would be stupid too. You just cannot think when you've got nothing to eat.

She says he literally starved her – but then says she prepared their dinners, which surely must mean she could have scarfed down food when he wasn't looking. She says she was allowed to eat the cakes that his mother baked on her weekend trips. She had her own fridge with its own comestibles in it and, as she was capable of teaching herself high German, handicrafts, science and other subjects, it seems unthinkable that she would not have also been able to learn what kind of nutrition she needed and to get it from him: after all, she wheedled most other concessions from him, including, eventually, the right to venture outside. Could she not have asked for, and got, more than the tinned and frozen foods that she has since told investigators they lived on?

That Priklopil aided her in her schooling cannot be denied. Superintendent Sabine Freudenberger was the first to speak with Natascha after she freed herself. She said: 'Natascha has a huge vocabulary; the kidnapper taught her, gave her books. He also told her that he had chosen her. If he hadn't taken her on that day, he would have caught her another day.'

It was only in 2006 that Priklopil decided to grant Natascha the ultimate concession, day-release from his ordered and closed universe into an outside world that he had for so long painted bleaker than a starless sky. Priklopil had reached a stage in his disturbed mind where he considered Natascha to be a 'proper' girlfriend.

It was the beginning of the end of everything.

The parallels between the John Fowles novel *The Collector* and Natascha's situation have been mentioned before and, at the time of writing, police confirm that they are still trawling through Priklopil's possessions to see if he read this book or used it as any kind of blueprint for what he did. Even as Priklopil prepared to step out into the real world with Natascha – the world he had deliberately retreated from in order to enjoy his illicit life with his captive – the thoughts that his captive has mirror exactly those of Miranda Grey in the Fowles book.

Natascha says she dreamed of attacking Priklopil with an axe, and that is the very way Fowles's heroine Miranda attacks the nerdy, obsessive Frederick Clegg; the real girl and the fictional girl, both kept in dungeons, took on the female role of making shopping lists, and both are concerned about the plight of the starving in the world. In her diary, Fowles's Miranda writes: 'There is a sort of relationship between us. I make fun of him. I attack him all the time but he senses when I'm "soft" . . . so we slip into teasing states that are almost friendly. It's partly because I'm so lonely . . . part weakness, part cunning, and part charity. But there's a mysterious fourth part I can't define. It can't be friendship. I loathe him.'

That complexity of feeling was apparent in Natascha from the first time she spoke of her captor. Fowles said of his fictional captive: 'Knowing somebody automatically makes you feel close to him. Even when you wish he was on another planet.' Miranda is so lonely that she wants her captor to come to her, saying: 'I had a feeling . . . of the most peculiar closeness to him – not love or attraction or sympathy in any way. But linked destiny. Like being shipwrecked on an island – a raft – together.'

Yet when he came to Natascha, to take her out, parade her like a girlfriend so she could boost his ego the way steroids boost a weightlifter's muscles, Priklopil was laying the foundations for the destruction of the world he cherished. He had duped himself into thinking that being bonded together by circumstance was genuine love and affection, when it was only ever an accommodation to get by. It was his Achilles heel and would, ultimately, kill him.

It was after her eighteenth birthday on 17 February 2006 that he began taking her with him to shops and museums, having warned her that he was heavily armed and wired with explosives. If she made any attempt to attract attention, he said, he would blow both of them up.

At the time of writing the Austrian police are following up 30 sightings of Natascha in public with Priklopil. In restaurants, in supermarkets, in the DIY chain store Hornbach, in his car, in his garden and on the streets near his home. This plethora of sightings has contributed to a growing speculation in Austria – one that manifested itself a month after she was freed in a particularly virulent e-mail campaign against her – that she could in fact have escaped at virtually any time and simply chose not to.

She was held back, however, by the knowledge of what her captor was capable of, what she thought him capable of. 'We are not Natascha and we should not judge her,' said one psychiatrist. 'She knew him, she knew her own fears. We do not: we were not there.'

Priklopil, the loner, the mummy's boy, the tormented wretch who fitted in nowhere, who nurtured a sick obsession until it took his sanity, kept Natascha in line with threats of violence. It would take a very special person to break such a grip. Someone like Natascha Kampusch.

A school picture of Natascha taken in the last year before she vanished when she was rumoured to have been unhappy at home.

Natascha aged four, in 1992, when this picture was taken of her for a calendar, which her father kept throughout the long years of her imprisonment.

This is the photo from the passport that she happened to have with her when she was seized in 1998. That fact led the police investigation in numerous wrong directions.

The run-down Rennbahnweg housing estate where Natascha lived with her mother and from where she was kidnapped on her way to school.

A typical little girl's bedroom, but Natascha spent many hours alone here. Her mother kept it untouched from the day Natascha disappeared.

The block of flats where Priklopil used to live and where his mother still lived until she was forced to go into hiding by the tumultuous events of August 2006.

Priklopil's BMW was his pride and joy. This is the car that Natascha was cleaning when she seized her chance to escape.

The warehouse where Priklopil and his friend Ernst Holzapfel based their renovations business.

The 'Wanted' picture of Wolfgang Priklopil, issued by police in the immediate aftermath of Natascha's escape and just hours before he committed suicide.

Christine's Schnellimbiss, the snack bar that Natascha's parents and Priklopil all visited and that may have provided a link between Natascha and her kidnapper.

The junction at Melangasse and Rennbahnweg in Vienna, close to her school gates, from where Natascha was snatched by Priklopil.

The white van that was used in the kidnapping, parked in a police yard. This vehicle provided the only concrete lead in the case, but it didn't yield a result.

The sign at the town limits of Strasshof that Natascha was driven past by her kidnapper on the way to the cellar where she would spend the next eight years of her life.

In the aftermath of her daughter's disappearance, Natascha's mother Brigitta Sirny displays one of the police missing posters put up across the capital.

GESUCHT

KAMPUSCH Natascha;

Seit 2.3.1998, 07.00 Uhr, ist die 10-jährige KAMPUSCH Natascha abgängig. Sie wurde zuletzt beim Ekazent Wien 22., Rennbahnweg Nr. 27, auf dem Weg zur Schule gesehen.

Personsbeschreibung:

135-140 cm groß, etwas pummelig, schulterlange hellbraune Haare, bekleidet mit weinroter Nylonjacke, Kleid (Oberteil Jeansstoff, Unterteil blau/weiß kariert), hellblauen Wollstrümpfen, schwarzen Schuhen, hellblaue Kunststoffbrille, trug Schulrucksack (türkis mit gelben Deckel).

Fragen:

1.) Wer hat Natascha seit dem 2.3.1998, 07.00 Uhr, gesehen?
2.) Wer kann Angaben über ihren Aufenthalt machen?
3.) Wer kann Angaben die mit der Abgängigkeit von Natascha in Zusammenhang stehen könnten?

Hinweise bitte an das Sicherheitsbüro
Tel.: 31346/36130 od. 36072,
sowie jede andere Polizeidienststelle

The missing poster that was posted on the Internet as the hunt for Natascha went international and fears grew she had been sold into the child sex trade.

Wolfgang Priklopil's seemingly unremarkable home, where Natascha spent 3,096 days locked in a cellar.

The stairs from the garage leading down to a small workshop where there was a concealed entrance to Natascha's dungeon.

Priklopil's system of concealment was virtually foolproof. This is the cupboard in front of the hidden entrance.

The last of four doors that leads from the antechamber to the tiny dungeon. One of the four cellar doors nearly severed Priklopil's finger in the early days of Natascha's imprisonment.

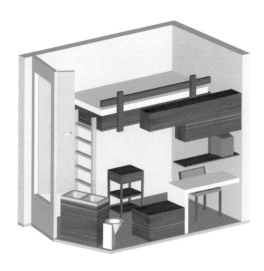

Plan of the cellar dungeon

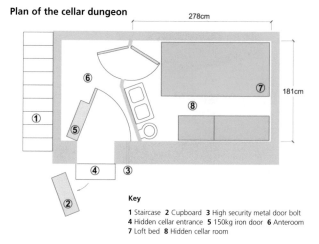

278cm

181cm

① ⑥ ⑤ ④ ③ ② ⑦ ⑧

Key

1 Staircase **2** Cupboard **3** High security metal door bolt
4 Hidden cellar entrance **5** 150kg iron door **6** Anteroom
7 Loft bed **8** Hidden cellar room

A graphic representation of Natascha's hidden dungeon home. The uniquely horrifying nature of her ordeal has been constantly stressed by all those who have been involved in the case.

View from the entrance to the cellar room showing
Natascha's elevated bed.

The day before she
was kidnapped,
Natascha had told a
friend she dreamed
of having her own
writing desk, not
knowing how soon
she would get her
wish.

A tiny space at the end of the hidden room was Natascha's bathroom and toilet with no barrier between it and the living area where she passed the time.

Over the years, Priklopil bought Natascha clothes, books and toys. But despite the clutter, this could never be a normal teenager's bedroom.

Aerial view of the house showing the rear garden with the disused swimming pool (white circle) where Priklopil grew tomatoes and the rear garage with white van parked outside it. The green square just below that is a plastic sheet on which soil from the garden was placed for forensic analysis.

The last image of Wolfgang Priklopil, recorded by a CCTV camera on the day of Natascha's escape, shortly before he committed suicide.

At about the same time, Natascha is led from the Donaustadt police station under a blanket. She is wearing the dress and ballet slippers she escaped in and the marks on her legs are clearly visible.

Natascha's horrific ordeal and dramatic escape were front page news in Austria for weeks and the story quickly became an international phenomenon.

Natascha's first TV interview was the most viewed programme of all time in Austria with over 2.7 million viewers, or 80 per cent of the market.

Natascha's dad Ludwig Köch with a copy of one of the first pictures taken of his daughter after her extraordinary reappearance.

Her mother Brigitta Sirny with a picture of her daughter after learning she had been freed.

Natascha, her mum (in the red suit) and other family members go flat hunting. The return to normal life will be long and potentially difficult, even for someone as exceptionally resilient and courageous as Natascha Kampusch.

5

Trails Leading to Nowhere

It has been described as the most disgraceful police operation in Austria since the post-war republic was founded. Natascha Kampusch's disappearance triggered the biggest hunt the country had ever known. But it was a deeply flawed one, full of missed opportunities, blunders, even at times a lack of enthusiasm. More than one commentator has remarked that perhaps the authorities might have done more if they had been searching for a well-to-do child instead of one from a sinkhole estate and a broken home. Whatever the reasons, the Kampusch case will be debated long into the future and will be seen as the benchmark for how not to conduct a MISPER – missing person's – investigation.

Until she was found, Austrian police had always maintained the operation had been a textbook one, with every lead followed and every clue carefully scrutinised. The missing girl was certainly high profile; at one stage she was in seventh place on the international police agency Interpol's top 10 of missing children. Interpol

Austria chief Herbert Beuchert insisted: 'We have tried everything. The child abuser rings in the Netherlands, the corresponding website on the Internet. But we could not find a substantial lead anywhere. No suspicious connections. Nothing.'

Another detective, Rudolf Koenig, said: 'There is no comparable case of a missing person that has seen such effort during the investigation. We really did everything humanly possible.' But did they? The facts suggest a series of missed opportunities and wild goose chases. The police even visited the kidnapper's home, stood yards from where their quarry was hidden. They failed ever to suspect the quiet loner.

The first the public knew of the story was when the Austrian Press Agency APA carried a brief report on 3 March, one day after Natascha vanished. It said: 'A 10-year-old girl went missing yesterday, Monday, in Vienna-Donaustadt. After the girl did not come home in the evening, the parents called police. Natascha Kampusch did not go to school or the after-school kindergarten. Police inquiries during the course of the evening were unsuccessful.'

The final sentence is one that could be applied to the whole eight-plus years of Natascha's ordeal.

Although she was snatched some time between 7 and 8 a.m. on Monday 2 March 1998, the first police knew of the disappearance was when Natascha's mother turned up at the police station on Rennbahnweg at 5.30 p.m., some ten hours later.

Officers on the reception desk told her they were unable to take missing person reports and diverted her to a different police station where such reports could be logged. As a result she was sent instead to the Donaustadt police station. There the mother was taken to an interview room where a report was written up and dispatched to the Vienna Sicherheitsbüro [security office], an organisation which has since been disbanded and which has borne the brunt of the criticism over missed opportunities in the Kampusch case.

In police circles, as well as to the public, the Sicherheitsbüro was known simply as the SB, or Berggasse, after the street where it is located. It was designed as an élite crime-fighting unit to tackle serious crimes, created to mirror the Sureté in France, and it regarded itself as the flagship of the Austrian police force, comparable with the FBI in America or Scotland Yard in the UK. But, unlike Scotland Yard and the FBI, Austrian police were rarely equipped with even computer facilities, and even when police officer Sabine Freudenberger, who was one of the first to interview the girl, gave her now famous interview with the ORF on Natascha's release, a typewriter could be seen in the background.

This, in September 2006. Was it a symbol of the antiquated methods used to try to solve the case?

The SB had been created in the times of the Austro-Hungarian empire. The Berggasse in the Alsergrund district of Vienna where it is based was also the street where the father of psychoanalysis Sigmund Freud once had his offices. The SB was located in a sprawling nineteenth-century brick-built military barracks at the end of the street near the Danube canal – designed by an architect who killed himself after he realised he had forgotten to include toilets in the design.

As Natascha's mother outlined what she knew of her daughter's disappearance at the Donaustadt police station, the missing ten-year-old had already been in the cellar for twelve hours.

By the next day, 3 March, a 12-year-old girl who went to the same school told her mother she had seen Natascha being pulled into a white minivan and that she thought the abductor had a helper. The information was not made public for another two weeks when the statement was released to the media on 19 March. In the intervening period the girl was debriefed by detectives and a search instigated for the kind of white vehicle the girl had managed to describe.

At the same time Wolfgang Priklopil was heading back from the Korneuberg Hospital after having his middle finger stitched, the result of his accident with his 150-kilo door guarding the entrance to Natascha's prison.

In Donaustadt, where the search was most intense, officers put out an appeal for witnesses who might have seen something, and questioned family, school-friends and locals to build up a picture of the youngster's last known movements. A large number of policemen were on the streets near her home, interrogating passers-by and scouring the route to school for clues. A child's pullover found on the street near where she was taken was found and rushed to her parents for identification, but was quickly ruled out as not belonging to Natascha.

Two more people contacted the police claiming to

have seen her. One said she had been on a No. 37 tram, while another claimed to have seen her shopping in a supermarket in Vienna's 23rd district. Natascha's family can believe the latter; they say she enjoyed shopping, so more officers were dispatched to look for signs of the missing girl in the Donauzentrum shopping centre, named as one of her favourite spots.

The police seemed to set some store by the fact that Natascha had vanished with her passport on her, fuelling the suggestion that she might have run away after the row with her mother. As a consequence, Austrian police informed their Hungarian colleagues through Interpol.

The statement of the child witness who claimed to have seen her being taken into a van was also scrutinised in detail, especially after police received an anonymous tip-off about a white minivan from Strasshof that matched the description of the vehicle they were looking for.

On the day of the disappearance, a decision was taken to follow every possible link to any van owners. There were 700 white vans, registered all over the country, that matched the description given by the witness. Their owners, including the kidnapper, were all traced, interviewed and crossed off the suspect list.

It was two weeks after Natascha's abduction that police finally got around to questioning the then 36-year-old Priklopil. Two weeks in which he was able to prepare his explanation for having the van, and to have his answers to possible police questions carefully rehearsed.

Asked where he was on the morning of 2 March, he

said: 'I was alone at home.' Police said later that they had taken this at face value. Austrian police spokesman Gerhard Lang described Priklopil eight years later as 'convincing, friendly and co-operative' and added, 'There seemed no reason to doubt his claims.' He said they had taken pictures of his van in which they found building debris and tools.

They did not, however, photograph Priklopil. The private detective Walter Poechhacker, who worked on the case for eight years, says the decision was incomprehensible. He said: 'Even the simple decision to take a snap of the 700 suspects might have brought the matter to a speedy conclusion.' He went on: 'They had in their hands at least one person who clearly claimed to have seen the kidnapping, and who was later proven quite correct in what she said. Think of what a difference it might have made if they had photographed the kidnapper along with the others who were on the suspect list, and if they had shown it to those who claimed to have witnessed the kidnapping! But they never did this.'

The police defended the way Priklopil slipped through their fingers by saying they did the best they could with 700 people to interview, but Poechhacker refused to accept this: 'Even if they did not want to photograph the people they interviewed, why did they not take a police sniffer dog along when questioning Priklopil? They might well have discovered the small child hidden in the cellar. The dog might have gone crazy if it had been allowed to sniff in the van. Why not?'

When officers turned up at the kidnapper's home to

question him and to search his minivan, they were quick to dismiss him as a suspect – this despite the fact that his relatively new vehicle was covered in building site dirt and dust, a fact that might have led a police officer to wonder whether the suspect had been burying evidence, or a body.

When interviewed on the doorstep, his prize safely concealed yards from where the policemen stood, Priklopil claimed he used the people carrier to transport building materials to and from properties he renovated.

And that was that. A single man, living alone, no girlfriends, but he was instantly dismissed in an interview that took less than four minutes. And neither then nor subsequently did they ask to search his premises.

In the light of everything that has occurred since 23 August 2006, Austrians are starting to ask why police did not search Priklopil's house then, and why, during an eight-and-a-half-year investigation that never led anywhere, they did not consider going back to the home in Strasshof with a search warrant. Natascha case detective Dr Ernst Geiger said: 'What should we have done? We couldn't search the houses of 700 people and prise open their cellars without concrete suspicions. Legally, it would have been impossible.'

He added that it was Priklopil's façade of normality that worked in his favour: he had no previous offences and did not appear suspicious. He was calm and polite when the officers interviewed him and seemed, according to them, as if he had 'nothing to hide'.

Just one week after Natascha went missing Detective

Hannes Scherz from the SB had expressed the frustration of his men. 'Our hope that the child disappeared "voluntarily" and will reappear somewhere alive diminishes by the day. We have absolutely no leads on this girl whatsoever.'

This was hearty news indeed to the owner of No. 60 Heinestrasse as he tuned into the press conference on the radio.

Critics say the policemen who went to see Priklopil should have spoken with neighbours, from whom they would have heard about the whacky security devices that peppered his home, his lack of girlfriends, his apparent mother fixation. Could have, should have, would have – hindsight has become the watchword of the Natascha Kampusch case.

Instead, in those first weeks, the focus shifted wildly to the city of Graz, 200 kilometres away, where a released child murderer lived. He had no white van.

'Often police have to act on intuition: either you feel something or you don't. Ultimately criminologists have to rely on coincidences,' said Dr Geiger, but added that the fact that they had been so close to solving the case more than eight years ago and didn't was 'very, very unsatisfactory'.

Nonetheless, efforts were made, even if they were misdirected. Huge numbers of officers were deployed on the streets of the capital, while in neighbouring Hungary, Interpol alerted officers there to be on the watch for Natascha. It was her favourite place, and perhaps the unhappiness she felt at home had tipped her over the edge and she had decided to flee there.

'Hell is breaking loose here,' said Scherz, of the situation in Austria as the leads started to come in and were one by one checked and ruled out. 'We constantly get new leads,' he said, 'but none has really been viable so far.' In fact, three weeks into the investigation, 300 leads had already been followed, all of them ultimately fruitless, all leading nowhere.

In Vienna a month after Natascha vanished the search was upgraded, and became the biggest missing persons investigation in the city's history when hundreds of officers and volunteers joined up in a last push to explore every unexplored avenue. Police divers from the WEGA (Vienna Action Squad A) searched lakes and the Danube, ten police dogs were used for scouring the island called 'Donauinsel', and there was support in the water from ships of the Danube Service and the federal police.

They also searched all the neighbouring lakes and streams, without success. Police helicopters were fitted with special infra-red detection equipment, so that local woods could also be searched. Hundreds of officers fanned out as far as the Czech border nearly 130 kilometres away. Their counterparts across the frontier joined in, with Czech police carrying out inquiries in Prague and sending alerts across the country. Vienna's 21st and 22nd districts were divided into sixteen sectors in total and assigned foot patrols with dogs. All abandoned buildings were searched, and 20,000 people quizzed.

Nothing.

On 6 April the search was downsized, but police pledged to carry on, opening a Natascha Taskforce office involving dozens of officers, a search that was still in operation, on a smaller scale, in August 2006, the week she came back to life.

On 13 April came a new clue. A married couple reported to the police that they saw a white van in Rennbahnweg at the time when Natascha disappeared. 'The van is believed to have a licence number plate from Gänserndorf ("GF"). At least the G is certain,' according to now Lieutenant-Colonel Gerhard Haimeder of Criminal Direction 1 of the Vienna police force.

Gänserndorf, north of Vienna, includes the suburb of Strasshof where Priklopil lived. Even this did not instigate a return visit to No. 60 Heinestrasse.

In Austria, as in England, as in Zambia or Zimbabwe, the longer a child remains missing, the more a MISPER investigation turns slowly into a murder inquiry. 'That we have still not found a solid trace of Natascha after four weeks greatly concerns me,' said Haimeder.

The next step for police was the murky netherworld of child molesters and paedophiles. A list of twenty major suspects was drawn up, all guilty of child abduction or assault in the recent past. All had an alibi for the time Natascha went missing.

One man called the SB saying he was holding Natascha and wanted a million schillings in ransom. He called again and, while officers kept him talking, an armed team was dispatched as technicians rapidly traced the call. He turned out to be an alcoholic loser trying to cash in. Instead of a ransom he ended up with a jail sentence.

What set the Natascha case apart from other child abduction incidents was the complete and utter lack of clues after the initial disappearance. Haimeder from the Sicherheitsbüro called it 'highly unusual'. Struggling children usually drop possessions or their pleas are heard. Apart from the sighting of her being pulled inside the van there was a distinct lack of forensic evidence. Haimeder added: 'With all the resources at our disposal we have nothing. No traces, no clothes have been found, nothing.'

After the suspect from Graz was eliminated from police inquiries, the focus switched back once more to the child witness who saw the white van. The twelve-year-old girl who claimed to have seen Natascha getting into it was interviewed again at length. She said she saw Natascha around 7.15 a.m. near the round-about in Melangasse with a white van on the right-hand side of the road. The girl stated that the van appeared to be rather new, and had a high roof, dark side windows, and a single back window. As Natascha walked past the vehicle, one of two people reached out and pulled her inside.

She spent many hours with police, who trawled through manufacturers' brochures finding different models of vans. The girl identified the van she saw as a 'Ford Transit-ish' – what Priklopil actually had was a Mercedes, a vehicle similar enough in appearance to merit him the visit from the police.

Hannes Scherz, meanwhile, was increasingly convinced there was something wrong with the picture he was getting: 'I have never experienced anything like it, something is wrong,' he said. 'It is very rare that children of Natascha's age run away from home. And if they do, they come back after a few days. And if it should be a sex crime, the site of the crime is usually close to the home of the victim.'

Well, Priklopil was indeed only a short car journey away.

'Natascha's family informed us that she never went off with strangers,' Scherz added. Could the family themselves be behind the disappearance of Natascha? The question that had become the chatter of Vienna's pubs and cafés was put to him in a newspaper interview. He replied: 'Of course we also considered that. But the father has been absolutely eliminated from the suspect list.' About the mother he was less emphatic, but said: 'She does not seem to have anything to do with it. At least, we don't have any clues.'

Hans Girod, a criminology professor at the University of Berlin, speculated at the time about the profile of the possible kidnapper:

In 80 per cent of cases the offenders are relatives, acquaintances, intimate partners, spouses or friends. Although exceptions are entirely possible, there is a rule of thumb: the more perfectly the kidnapping was executed, the closer the relationship is between the offender and the victim.

Prominent distinctive features in such cases are the active participation of the offender in the search for the missing person, putting up missing persons adverts or putting about self-accusations in a circle of close friends.

The *Kurier* newspaper introduced a new factor into the investigation when it hired the private detective Walter Poechhacker, a move that instantly put him at odds with the SB, who saw it as a public insult that they had hired a single man to do the work of their agency. After he had investigated it for a week, the newspaper paid him off but, convinced there was more to be found, he then carried on working on the case for free, and asked for his newspaper fee to be paid to the St Anna Children's Hospital in Vienna. Poechhacker told the authors:

> I had worked on nine missing children cases, and this was my tenth. I had solved all the other nine, and as soon as I started looking at it I was convinced that someone within the family or the community was involved. It just doesn't happen that a child can vanish so completely and effectively if a complete stranger is involved. Such a clean disappearance only comes with careful planning and with someone who knows what and who they are looking for.

He admits that initially he suspected the father, but after talking to friends he soon realised there had been a strong bond of love between the two. Numerous people told him how happy Natascha had been with her father, and how much she enjoyed her time with him.

In a newspaper article, Poechhacker wrote: 'All the evidence points to a kidnapping, that the answer to this case lies in the immediate environment of Natascha. If all those concerned were tested with a polygraph or lie-detector test, then the answer would quickly become clear.'

Convinced that a lie-detector test might settle the case and prove his theory that a member of the family was involved, Poechhacker invited a German professor to Vienna to test five principal suspects, including the mother and father. The £5,000 cost of the tests he paid out of his own money. But the procedure did not go as well as he had hoped: 'The professor, who was 81 years old, was late getting here, and could only interview three candidates. The other two candidates had to be inter-viewed the next day.'

But he was particularly unhappy that it was not the professor but an assistant who had questioned the mother. He later learned that, in any case, the scientist's work was discredited after he gave evidence that helped get a US soldier stationed in Germany convicted for murdering his wife, only for the real murderer to be found a month later. 'It was really a shame that we had him and not someone else. Who knows what might have been uncovered at this point?'

Nonetheless, Poechhacker believes the exercise was not completely flawed. He claims that it revealed that there was one person connected to the family who was clearly guilty of something. He said: 'One person who was tested was in a nervous state the like of which I have never before witnessed. That person smoked non-stop, their hands shook, and when I looked into their eyes we both knew what the other was thinking. I thought we were going to get a confession at that point.' He refused to say who that person was.

After the tests were carried out Poechhacker had offered to give the results and the interview tapes to the police, but claims there was little of interest in them. The original lie-detector tests were carried out on 19 December 1998, and the tapes in fact remained with the detective until 28 February 2001, when he offered them again and the Natascha task force finally accepted them.

In a book he wrote on the case, Poechhacker states that he believes that the mother's lovers and associates were not properly investigated by the police.

In television and newspaper appearances she [Frau Sirny] made an impressive figure, in contrast to Herr Koch, who seemed somewhat helpless and lost for words. She had a Madonna statue in her flat that was always in the background as she spoke about her daughter. There was a photo of Natascha next to it. She would explain to people who said she seemed cold that she merely seemed tough, and reserved her tears for the privacy of her own four walls.

One question that has not been properly answered remains: how strong were the connections between Frau

Sirny, her married lovers including Ronnie Husek, and Wolfgang Priklopil, who all drank in the same bar over the years?

The detective Poechhacker was convinced throughout his work on the case that police were trying to deflect him from investigating Natascha's mother and the men around her. He wrote in his book that he got the impression that there was 'pressure from above' for detectives 'not to investigate in this direction'.

He says in his book that he stated quite clearly to police that it was his impression that all lines of inquiry relating to Brigitta Sirny were being closed down. He added that Max Edelbacher, chief of the SB from 1988 to 2002, when it was scrapped and he was demoted, had admitted in a telephone conversation that there was 'resistance' in the Natascha task force to investigating Frau Sirny's connections, but he alone was unable to change it.

'I sympathise with him,' said Poechhacker, ' but I do not understand why, if he is head of the SB, he didn't simply just say to them, do it. I believe by this point there were already orders from above telling them to cover their mistakes by hook or by crook.'

At one point Poechhacker wrote to the Austrian Home Office to complain about the lack of progress and enthusiasm in the Natascha case, but nothing was done. He also suggested that senior detectives who were part of the investigation might not have been too keen to have a scandal erupting as they climbed the promotional ladder. In particular he named Edelbacher and

Geiger, who at one time were both short-listed to head the new élite police force formed from the disbanded rump of the SB.

Geiger, 51, was head of the Homicide Commission of the Vienna SB from 1991 until 2002, and then became head of the Criminal Police Department. In 2005 he was decorated with a silver medal for merits in serving the country, but early in 2006 he was given a suspended three-month sentence for tipping off pimps about impending police raids on their illegal brothels.

Natascha's mother meanwhile showed she was well capable of using the media to further her cause. At one point she triggered a huge debate across the country after she told the local public broadcaster the ORF that her family allowance for Natascha had been stopped just over a week after she vanished. She said: 'They told me where there is no child there is no money.' The family minister even got involved at one point, and messages of support from the public came flooding in, with offers of money to aid in the search for Natascha.

She also started a campaign of criticism of the SB for daring to suggest that a poor mother could be involved in the disappearance of her daughter. Her interview with one newspaper sparked a campaign against this police line of inquiry.

The police probe included questioning two of her married lovers. This infuriated the men in question, as, according to Poechhacker, they were terrified their wives would find out. One had been pulled out of his local pub and invited to allow police to search his flat, which he had agreed to as his wife was away at the time. They also tried to find a third man but never succeeded.

One of the other two, Ronnie Husek, is understood to have spent the weekend with Brigitta Sirny before Natascha vanished. He was known to be wealthy and it is believed he was the source of the funding that Frau Sirny had spoken about with Frau Glaser when she said she expected to start up in business again shortly.

With Natascha still missing and the finger-pointing increasing, the pressure on her parents also increased, and with no love lost between them they started blaming each other for the girl's disappearance.

The accusations had first started on 22 March 1998, when Natascha's mother told local newspaper *Kronen Zeitung* that on trips to Hungary the father had been in the habit of taking Natascha to nightclubs that in Austria you would need to be over 21 to visit. She said: 'I asked him how an adult person could be so stupid as to take a ten-year-old child into a disco where go-go girls were performing.'

Hungary was quickly ruled out as a crime scene. Not only did Natascha's schoolfriends, interviewed by police officers, emphasise how much she spoke of enjoying the time she spent there, but in addition, one hundred Hungarian officers had searched the village where Natascha's father owned a house and questioned neighbours. The house itself was put under observation. Neighbours set up patrols and one policeman was stationed there. The result was they believed her father was telling the truth and had no idea where his daughter was.

For his part Natascha's father, tormented with grief and not enjoying the best of relations with his ex, became convinced his wife was involved, and made a claim accusing her of involvement in their daughter's abduction. He later retracted it, and when Natascha was finally found, apologised. He said: 'The main thing is my little girl is back, anything else is unimportant. I don't want to create any bad feeling.'

Natascha's face then, as now, was all over Vienna as the increasingly desperate search dragged on. She stared out from posters plastered all over the capital. Her image was even pinned up in Christine's truck-stop bar, no doubt giving Priklopil some strange satisfaction when he called in there for his apple juice and sausage snack.

She featured on an Austrian version of *Crimewatch* called *Aktenzeichen XY Ungeloest* or 'Cases XY Unsolved', during which a member of the public called in to say they had spotted Natascha in a car with Hungarian licence plates.

'If we had a crime scene, it would be much easier,' bleated Haimeder of the SB. After a summit in the Sicherheitsbüro the night before, police decided to change their strategy. 'The time of big searching operations is over,' he declared. The police were to switch to more detailed, smaller swoops.

Natascha's parents reported that people continued to approach them, claiming to have seen their daughter. One man called repeatedly, asserting that he lived in Langenzersdorf and then also in Gänserndorf. 'He said that he had kidnapped Natascha because she reminded him of his deceased daughter. That would fit the clues claiming our child had been driven away in a bus with Gänserndorf plates,' said Ludwig. The capacity that other people had to play cruel mind games with them left them wounded, astounded and exhausted.

In August of 1998 body parts found in Croatia caused a stir in Vienna when Interpol faxed the task force that the dismembered remains were those of a girl aged between ten and fourteen. The parents braced themselves for the worst, but the body was declared not to be that of Natascha within hours of paperwork and DNA samples being sent to Zagreb.

In October the search went into the realms of the paranormal. Chief Inspector Helmut Gross turned out a large contingent of officers to search a Second World War era ammunition depot where he was told by a psychic that Natascha was being held. Neither a living or a dead Natascha was discovered.

In December 1998 the task force was able to access a new computer system called VICLAS – the Violent Crime Linkage Analysis System – which recorded and compared behavioural patterns of offenders, including sex offenders. The programme also offered up probability theories on how likely it was that several crimes had been committed by the same offender. 'In the past, we would have needed weeks – even months – for this work,' said Thomas Mueller, head of the police psychological department. Mueller had worked on the cases of Franz Fuchs, the mad bomber, and Jack Unterweger, the serial killer, and was formerly head of the criminal psychology department of the SB – which consisted only of himself. His book *Beast Man* was Austria's bestselling book in 2004. The computer system was hailed as a break-through for detectives, but it had one flaw – it could only work if the perpetrator was in the system.

Wolfgang Priklopil had only ever had a speeding ticket and a telling-off for killing a sparrow. He was not on the radar.

Christmas came and went. Natascha's parents bought presents for her, wrapped them up and placed them under a tree in her home. The ceremony was a necessity for their psychological stability, a statement that they believed she was alive, not dead. This faith, in the face of all the signs that she was, probably, long dead, kept them sane.

Now the hunt was truly about to depart from this world to enter the next. Psychics who triggered one search would now play a far more prominent part in the hunt.

'We have had fortune-tellers contact us several times over the past years,' said SB chief Edelbacher, 'but never quite as many as now.' From the thousand-plus tips the Natascha task force had received about her disappearance, every tenth one came from what he termed the 'fourth dimension'.

On an official level police said they were none to happy with the deluge of information from Ouija board shufflers, soothsayers and crystal fondlers. Unofficially, said Edelbacher, 'In the Natascha case we do not want to leave anything untried. After all, we've all got kids of our own.'

Thus it was that three officers of the narcotics squad were assigned to deal specifically with psychic sightings of Natascha Kampusch in their spare time. They were known as 'Department X-Files' among colleagues in the Vienna force.

Of the dozens of psychics who were either consulted by family or volunteered their services, one stands out. Clairvoyant Haller was asked to take part in a discussion about the case by the Austrian state broadcaster ORF, nearly a year after Natascha went missing. Haller had first become involved when she was contacted by police, but has refused to name the high-ranking officer who she alleges turned up at her home for advice.

The prediction she gave on television was the same one which she had given to the police and which turned out to be uncannily accurate. She told listeners how she could detect the 'energy of Natascha in the north-east of Vienna, past the pond for bathing in Hirschstetten' – which lay between where Natascha was kidnapped and where she was imprisoned in the cellar.

She also saw railroad tracks: Priklopil's home was next to one of Vienna's largest railway depots. She also spoke about a bar that the kidnapper used to frequent. She described it as a simple, one-storey, typical bar in the suburbs with loose chippings in the front. At the door there is one step and an old wooden floor, and 'something' inside was green – she was not sure if it was the door or the chairs.

Christine's bar, where Priklopil is suspected of first seeing Natascha, is also a simple one-storey affair in the style of dozens of similar bars across the city, with stone chips outside and a single step leading inside, but it is yellow not green.

Haller added: 'I saw the kidnapper as a slim man, around 40 years old.' The clairvoyant, now aged 61, still appears regularly on Austrian television and radio and in Austrian newspaper columns, and has worked as a clairvoyant for 40 years. That she foresaw that Natascha was located exactly where she was eventually found has not been commented on by police, who will also not confirm her claims that a senior member of the Natascha task force had approached the clairvoyant for help. It is therefore not known if he ever tried to match up the advice with files that might have shown Priklopil as a suspect from earlier in the investigation.

As well as mediums, cranks also appeared as the case captured the popular imagination. A former judge and Austrian presidential candidate, Martin Wabl, started his own investigation into the case and subsequently voiced allegations that the mother was involved in the disappearance of her daughter. But his claims lost their credibility when his belief became an obsession and Frau Sirny succesfully sued him for slander. He was eventually arrested for pretending to be a police officer in a bid to gather evidence to prove his case.

In 1999, their differences buried, the parents appealed for sponsors to come forward to contribute to a million-schilling fund – nearly 50,000 UK pounds – as a reward for people with information about Natascha's whereabouts. But the world, in its inevitable way, was moving on. Natascha remained an aura, a presence in the city and in the consciences of millions, but in time other figures – Joerg Haider, the late Princess Diana – became the front-page stories and in the lead items of the news shows.

The police admitted they were no nearer a solution than when the girl vanished a year before. 'We have not made any progress in this case compared to one year ago,' said Scherz on the first anniversary of Natascha's disappearance.

Another criticism of the police investigation was that no complete profile of a likely kidnapper was ever drawn up. Profiling, as developed in the FBI labs at Quantico in Virginia, is now used routinely by police forces all over the world. Psychiatric 'sketches' of the kind of man who might have taken her were attempted, but police sources told the authors that they were highly unsatisfactory.

The motives of sex offenders are very varied. Experts say they can be broken down into five categories – sex, power, anger, control and fear, in no particular order of prevalence. If a full profile of Priklopil had been drawn up it would have painted a picture of a loner, a man with a lot of time on his hands, a man who may have been an AMAC – a male abused as a child – and a man who had base views on women, who was probably a virgin, who needed to control.

And who owned a white van. If a full profile had been married to the white-van-man information, then it is a probability that the van owners who were visited in

Austria would have been looked at again and those fitting the bill of the profile would have been revisited.

It never happened.

One year on from the kidnapping, the Austrian police released this statement:

> We followed up 2,000 witness accounts, looked closely at 150 people, used 500 police officers, 200 gendarmes and 13 search dogs on various occasions, as well as the officers of the Danube patrol, and deployed search helicopters that spent a total of 150 hours in the air. We have arrived at our end. The possibility that Natascha was the victim of a crime is high. But we cannot rule out that she is still alive. Everything is possible.

The following month, after naked photos of a girl who had been missing for three years in Germany turned up on the Internet, investigators began probing the child pornography underbelly in Vienna. The city of Habsburg-ian elegance has its own seamy side of forced child prostitution and predators, warped souls preying on innocence. By the West Bahnhof rail station, and near the Prater park where the big wheel draws tourists, prostitution is rampant.

The homes of known paedophiles were raided, sickening images traded between criminals across Europe downloaded from their computers. Officers spent days comparing all images with those of Natascha. Several arrests were made. None of them had to do with Natascha.

Police thought that Natascha's kidnapper might be stealing children to order after a man tried twice in two weeks to snatch children in a Viennese suburb into his VW van. On the second occasion a girl bit him on the hand. The man was never caught.

One problem confronting investigators on the team was that every sexual assault, attempted abduction or abuse had to be scrutinised for links to Natascha. It meant weary and wasted hours of checks and cross-checks around the country. All the while Priklopil was less than 25 kilometres from the police HQ where his crime continued to baffle all those hunting him.

At one time a child molester was arrested in Lower Austria. It caused great excitement among the Natascha team, not least because a year before he was registered as living on the same street as her. He had a long record of child molestation, he was a loner, and he was a paedophile of the worst kind. He was also in prison for sex crimes on the day she was taken.

Police turned once more to the paranormal. 'I want the murderer of the child to be found,' said Franz Plasch, a pendulum operator who told the *Kronen Zeitung* with alarming authority: 'Natascha is dead. She was murdered on the second day of her disappearance.'

In front of Plasch, for the sake of the newspaper story, was spread a map of Vienna. The pendulum he dangled kept swinging towards a point in the north-east of the town. 'Here, near the so-called Kreuzlwiese, about 15 kilometres from the Stephansdom [St Stephen's Cathedral], lies the dead body. The murderer buried the girl about 25 centimetres deep in a section of the forest.'

Plasch could only point to an area within a radius of about 300 square metres. 'Unfortunately a more precise prediction is not possible. But I am confident that the police will find the dead body and release the parents from the pain of the uncertainty.' The police duly dispatched a search team with dogs. Of course, nothing was found, but Plasch was right in a few details: she was underground, she was north-east of the city and she wasn't far from St Stephen's Cathedral.

The new millennium arrived but brought no breakthrough in the case. In 2000 an officer said: 'Our knowledge has remained pretty much the same since 1998. We are sadly not any smarter than we were at the beginning.' Over 300 sites were checked in 1999 following indications that Natascha's body could have been buried at any one of them.

In 2001 the Internet was used for the first time in Austria in a missing person's case. A fully automated search machine, equipped with a photograph of Natascha, started rummaging through two million pages in the World Wide Web for the missing girl. The system of a German computer firm even digitally aged the face of Natascha. It was a slim hope, but a hope nonetheless.

Private enterprise came on board, too. The German computer corporation Cobion developed their own search engine machine designed to allow 1,000 computers to search all over the world for an image of Natascha. The help of the company, which usually searched for the criminal abuse of company logos and images, was welcomed.

In 2001, three years after she vanished, Ernst Geiger, one of the senior detectives in the investigation, said: 'The case is unique. It is the only example of a missing child under 14 who did not reappear – or turn up deceased – since the republic was founded in 1945.'

Natascha's father, still convinced that police were missing vital clues, devoted his efforts to working with Poechhacker in a relentless, all-consuming quest to find new evidence. The information he gave to officers led to several more digs in the area in an unsuccessful attempt to locate her body. For eight years neither of her parents gave up, despite the widespread belief among the public she was dead.

In 2002 the SB was disbanded, and suffered the insult of being merged with the local criminal investigation squad from which it had so long held itself haughtily aloof. But the Natascha case was not taken with the SB to its new home in the CID. Instead it became a 'cold case', the worst kind of all to work on, and the worst kind for parents who want results.

Under pressure from Poechhacker, an eight-man special commission of officers went back to reviewing all the files, witness statements, search material, and even tips, not just from this world but from the one beyond. A special commission of the local police squad mainly consisting of investigators from Burgenland, was set up, with their first task to go through the 140-page report and folders of evidence amassed in the previous four years by the private detective Poechhacker.

But although the team from the Natascha task force ploughed through thousands of pages, the original suspects and witnesses were not re-interviewed.

Poechhacker tells of his frustration and the repeated false leads. He said that at one point he and Koch had been planning to speak to friends of Koch's from local bars, because he knew some of them had seen Natascha. He said the questioning was called off when Frau Sirny called the pair of them to demand that they investigate a new lead which turned out to go nowhere.

Koch had tried to say no, but she called him again an hour later and talked him into it. Poechhacker said: 'Without Herr Koch it was obviously difficult for me to gain access to the circle of people in the community.'

Five years into Natascha's imprisonment the officers on the case were rotated again as a matter of principle. All unsolved murder cases are continually reviewed and new officers, it was felt, came to the Natascha case free of bias and sometimes 'able to see things that were originally overlooked by colleagues. And witnesses often have completely new motives after a few years. Lovers give alibis, ex-lovers take them.'

But nowadays there is a third important reason to dedicate time to these cold cases. Hannes Scherz said: 'Forensic science, especially the analysis of DNA through biological traces, has opened a whole new chapter with great chances over the last few years. The first thing we now do is look at the evidence that was collected at the time. Then we search for any traces, and finally we look at exactly what happened to that evidence.'

'Coincidence, that's what they are waiting for,' grumbled Poechhacker. 'Just like the murderer of school-girl Alex Schriefl, a famous case here in Austria, was discovered only after more than ten years when he got into a hassle with a police officer while drunk – just the same way they will solve the mystery of Natascha's disappearance. Only by coincidence.' He was nearly right.

But the cold case team did draw up a 50-page memorandum claiming that 'different people involved in the case at different times told different stories which, ultimately, did not add up.' Sources told the authors that they determined that 'in Natascha's surroundings there were people who had certain things to hide, petty crimes . . . that nonetheless might prove to have a connection to the disappearance of Natascha.' And so the investigation went back to square one with the re-interviewing of her family members, the van-spotters, the neighbours.

Everyone, it seems, aside from the loner in Strasshof who should have been ringing all sorts of alarm bells but wasn't. The Natascha case slid into a kind of legal torpor. Police went through the motions, appeals were made from time to time for new witnesses. Even a fresh set of photographs of the kind of clothes she wore on the day she went missing were made for Interpol and distributed around Europe.

General Roland Horngacher, a leading investigator on the case, said in despair: 'The Natascha Kampusch case is a police nightmare. We have done everything we can. But until we find new traces, or get new leads, this case simply cannot be closed.'

Horngacher was certainly in a position to comment but he was not a blameless figure. Between 1997 and 2002 he was head of the Wirtschaftspolizei, from 2002 to 2005 head of the Criminal Investigation Office, and from 2005 to 2006 head of the Vienna police. He was decorated with a Golden Medal of Merit for services to the country, but in 2006 he was suspended and at the time of writing was under investigation for abuse of office and accepting unauthorised gifts, and was also suspected of passing on confidential information to journalists.

By 2004 the focus had switched once more overseas. The police quizzed the French authorities regarding a possible connection to the case of child molester Michel Fourniret. The head of the Department of Investigations and Organised and General Crime of the Criminal Intelligence Service, Erich Zwettler, insists this is 'pure routine. There is no clue and no lead that there is any connection.' Fourniret stated that he often travelled abroad, using a white van. 'In Europe there are several thousand white vans, so you can hardly call this a lead,' Zwettler said.

In November of that year Poechhacker released his book *The Natascha Case*. In the foreword he expressed his frustration over the fact that a catalogue of blunders had meant a case that should have easily been solved had dragged on for years, and added: 'This book chronicles one of the biggest police scandals in modern Austrian history.'

Criticism has come from almost everyone who has been in a position to observe the investigation at close quarters. Dr Berger, who now plays such a pivotal role in trying to heal Natascha's mind, has been critical of the way the police handled the case, claiming they showed 'too much reticence', while prominent local editor Gerfried Sperl, in his column for the Vienna newspaper *Der Standard*, has said there are many questions that need to be asked of the police.

He asks: 'Why was Priklopil's house not at least put under observation, if for some reason a search warrant was not possible to get?' and goes on to ask how many of the 800 people currently officially missing in Austria, 200 of them children, are suffering fates similar to Natascha's, locked in dungeons while life goes on as normal above their heads.

The clearest summation of the failure of the investigation comes from one of its key players. Edelbacher was head of the Wiener Sicherheitsbüro at the time and only went into retirement the month before Natascha escaped. He said:

Nobody, not me nor any other policeman believed she could still be alive. This is a sensation. However, it is horrible that a girl could be held in our area for eight years while being unsuccessfully searched for by thousands of policemen. Questions, rightly, must be asked about where we went wrong. We thought about it so much and had so many theories, even that she had fallen into the hands of a child porn gang, everything. So many investigators gave their all, their heart's blood towards getting her back.

So, in the eight and a half years of the Natascha case, two policemen saw their careers ruined. The investigation failed on many levels. No search was made of Priklopil's home or van, either by officers alone or with dogs. No photograph was taken of him, no full profile drawn up. Police relied on a computer system that only charted known offenders, and the connection was seemingly never made between Christine's bar, the kidnapper and Natascha's family, all regulars there. It is not that the investigation lacked energy, but it did lack cohesiveness. It was misdirected, misspent and, ultimately, mismanaged.

6

Limited Freedom

The seasons passed. Natascha fretted about her elderly
grandparents and aunts. As her skin grew white her
mind stayed sharp. She thought of her growing nieces
and remembered fondly the holidays in Hungary. Her
vocabulary was improving by leaps and bounds, and
she was aware of a world much broader than the 160-
square-metre one she inhabited with Wolfi. The books,
the TV documentaries, the radio programmes – like
parchment soaking up spilled ink, Natascha drank in
information.

She had not yet earned a pass into that world she had
learned so much about. But on Natascha's eighteenth
birthday there was a celebration in the house. Police
sources said the two dined together and there was a
special cake afterwards which he bought from a con-
fectioner's some distance away from Heinestrasse. It's
understood that it was after the meal that he first
informed her that she had 'earned' the right to leave
the house with him. He began allowing her into the

garden, taking her to stores, and for walks, but always reminding her that he was heavily armed.

When she had escaped and a stunned world tried to comprehend the ghastliness of her experience, public opinion, ever fickle, turned against her precisely because of those rare trips into the outside world. The girl in the cellar suddenly took on the new and unwanted persona of the 'occasional prisoner', with over thirty sightings of her and Priklopil around Austria that the police said they were following up.

According to sources close to Natascha, who spoke on the condition of anonymity, when Natascha was sixteen or seventeen Priklopil eased his regime a little. She spoke of him becoming a little 'softer' on her. Some are of the opinion that he believed he could marry her at some stage, that his grooming of her had paid dividends: that she had fallen in love with him. 'The idea was obviously just a part of his deranged imagination,' said one of her inner circle.

By the time she was seventeen, however, he noticed that things were not going the way he expected them to, and he also realised her personality was becoming ever stronger. She told her advisers that he found her 'cheeky' and 'demanding'. The authors were told, despite the outings that were to come, that he hardened his regime during the final year together, that he hit her on occasion and sent her back to the dungeon when she was 'disobedient'. One adviser said:

Things got worse when he, I assume, grasped the certainty of his inevitable failure. He was not able to mould this child into the woman he wanted her to be; his sick experiment was totally unsuccessful. She is also very aware of that and that is why she thinks that he, in a way, gave her a chance to escape.

She told us that he would never ever allow her to be behind him; he always needed to keep an eye on her. But in the last stages of their time together he did start turning his back to her, and on the day of her escape he stayed like that for several minutes. That is when she ran for it. It could well be that, consciously or unconsciously, he wanted her to escape, to get rid of her.

During the period of limited freedom, Priklopil forced Natascha to help him with his house refurbishments, taking her to Hornbach. There she smiled at an employee who came and addressed her, but Priklopil sent him away. The same happened in a supermarket, where Natascha was dragged away by her captor when she started winking at another customer.

The residents of Strasshof remember having seen Priklopil often at the Chicken Grill takeaway, where he enjoyed his meal while Natascha stayed inside his BMW. Even Priklopil's nearest neighbour, Josef Jantschek, states that he saw Natascha 'more and more often' at the kidnapper's side. When he asked whether she was Priklopil's new girlfriend, Priklopil only replied that she was a girl from Yugoslavia working for him. Herr Jantschek said:

> I saw the young lady in the garden quite often over the past year. They also drove off together in his car, and every time she waved at us in a friendly way. When I asked who the young lady was he claimed she was a 'Yugoslav aide' he had 'borrowed' from a colleague to do some housework for him.
>
> We could not have known that it was the kidnapped Natascha Kampusch. When I asked him whether she was his new girlfriend, he only said no, she was doing work for him.

Natascha said she dared not try to raise the alarm with him: she truly believed Priklopil would murder the kindly old man without a second thought.

'You have to imagine what it was like, there just wasn't any time . . . he would have grabbed me, strangled me and killed Herr Jantschek. It was far too risky,' she would later say.

Another neighbour, Frau Stefan, 61, said: 'I saw him driving down our street with the girl twice recently. I also saw them walking down the main street once. My friend, another woman from the neighbourhood, also told me she saw them walking and holding hands.

'She looked very young, but seemed in a good mood and positive. We assumed they were a couple, we thought he had finally got himself a girlfriend.'

Natascha said Priklopil was tense every time they went out. She would later comment on how careful he was, hardly moving from her side. Ever the paranoid, Priklopil had panic attacks if she was just three centimetres distant from him, Natascha claims:

He wanted me to always walk in front of him and never behind. So that he could always keep an eye on me. And I couldn't go to anybody. He always threatened that he would do something to the people if I said anything to them. That he would kill them. And I couldn't risk that.

There were many people that I tried to give signs to, but people don't think of things like that. They don't read newspapers and think, 'Ah, this could be that girl that I read about . . .'

But generally there wasn't enough time. If I had made just one sound he would have pulled me away . . . and if that had been too late then he would have killed that person or me.

It was worse with the nice ones. Like the nice assistants in Baumarkt [a DIY store]. One asked me, 'Can I help you?' And I just stood there in a panic, uptight, with my heart beating fast and hardly able to breathe. And I could hardly move. And I had to helplessly watch as he got rid of the assistant. And I just had the chance to smile at the assistant because he was so friendly. I mean, he didn't know any better.

I always tried to smile a little bit like I did in the

old photos, in case anybody recognised my picture. But sometimes, at the beginning, I couldn't stand being around people. I wasn't used to it, and many people are discontented. It was very uncomfortable.

Natascha also recalled the weird mind games Priklopil played with her before they went out: 'Now and again, in his way, he gave me suggestions about how I could go behind his back and escape. This must have dawned on him within his paranoia. It was almost as if he wanted that some day I would be free. That things would go wrong, that somehow justice would win.'

The pair were frequently seen going shopping in supermarkets. Pensioner Hans Georg, 67, claims she winked at him during one of their shopping trips. He said: 'I thought to myself, something is wrong with her. I wanted to come up to them and ask what was the matter, but her companion took her by the hand and pulled her away. He gave me an evil stare.'

Natascha was also seen with Priklopil in another DIY shop, buying construction material and paint that was probably used during the time she was helping him renovate the flat in Vienna's 15th district that he wanted to rent out to immigrant Slavs in the area: the very flat he would be trying to lease to a prospective tenant who called on his mobile phone on the day of her escape.

As well as the outings, Natascha also won the right to choose the furniture of her cellar dungeon, so Priklopil took her to a furniture store and bought the things she selected. But the illusion of a normal life together would shatter at the most simple things. Priklopil was compulsively parsimonious. He would refuse to buy fresh bread until the last crust of the old one was eaten.

He even tried, sometimes successfully, to pass on his neurotic ideas to her. If she felt unwell he would deny her medicine and persuade her that they were all filled with 'heavy metals'. According to her advisers, the suggestion was implanted in her fragile mind so deeply, that she considers it to this very day. She scrutinises, for example, the content details on food can labels with the intensity of a microbiologist.

There were also more relaxing moments during their forced union, when she would help him tend the garden, plant roses or water the small vegetable patch next to the always empty pool. It would be a chance for her to enjoy the light of day, feel the fresh breeze on her pale skin and hear birds singing in the trees around her unlikely prison.

Gerhard Lang, head of the strategy department for the Federal Criminal Office who became a spokesman for the case after she freed herself, said:

There were a lot of videos and books in Priklopil's house. Many of the books were about the countryside, natural history and that sort of thing. The films were mostly the usual Hollywood movies you would see in any collection, the only thing I really remember is that *Mr Bean* was among them. There were also lots of recordings of news programmes that had obviously been edited to remove anything the kidnapper thought was unsuitable. She knew all about the introduction of the euro and was well informed about Austrian politics, for example. She got all that from the news programmes. Other things she taught herself from books. She learned how to knit from a book.

But reading, knitting and watching TV were interspersed with bouts of forced heavy labour, despite the fact that she was often weakened by what she said was the forced malnutrition that was part of her captor's bid to break her will. When Priklopil was building his second garage for the van he used to snatch her off the street, he made her carry heavy buckets filled with earth, as well as bulky construction material.

Despite her claims that she had one shot, and one shot only, at breaking loose, the opportunities for escape seemed, superficially, many and varied. One woman from Graz, over 200 kilometres away from Vienna, told police that Priklopil came to her house to repair her computer and that Natascha was waiting downstairs in his BMW for about an hour. She reportedly came down to her, opened the car door and asked her if she would like to come upstairs for a coffee, but Natascha politely declined and remained in the car.

'Our computer was broken,' the unnamed woman said, 'and a service man was sent from Lower Austria. When I saw the pictures of Herr Priklopil in the newspapers I recognised him straight away.'

She claims to have escorted Priklopil back to his car, where Natascha was sitting and waiting for him. The pensioner added, 'I told him then: "You have let your girlfriend wait for quite a long time." He just laughed and drove off.'

Ernst Holzapfel, the businessman who sold Priklopil a 24 per cent stake in his building renovation company for a little over 8,000 euros, also met her shortly before she took the decision to run.

Holzapfel, 42, was an interesting character to the police in the investigation. He was twice quizzed when the dungeon was discovered, the first time on the very day of Natascha's escape. However, he was cleared of having anything to do with the abduction and subsequent imprisonment of Natascha. His memory of meeting her parallels those of more casual acquaintances or passers-by: simply because no one could think the unthinkable of such a bland and seemingly asexual character as his associate, he too was fooled by him when he was within inches of Natascha.

Holzapfel, who would ultimately have to identify the corpse of his friend and colleague, was also the last person to speak with him alive. He said in a rather strained press conference shortly after Priklopil's death:

I first met Herr Priklopil during my time at Siemens in the eighties. We occasionally kept in touch after that. In the nineties he worked in my company and helped me out with the renovating and upgrading of real estate.

I have always thought that if one works with someone well over many years, one would get to know them well, too. That is why I am even more shocked about the events. I never noticed anything untoward throughout the whole time. Herr Priklopil behaved with me as usual. I would have never thought something as appalling as that would ever have been possible. I am bewildered over this appalling act. I would never have thought that he could have been a kidnapper.

I have never met any girlfriend of Herr Priklopil. Of course, we talked about his family and his mother and also about other trivial things, as is customary among good colleagues.

In recent years I occasionally visited his house in Strasshof, to pick up or bring back tools and machinery. Once I was in the garage and I saw the service pit from above. This was nothing unusual for me, because I knew that Herr Priklopil was often working on his cars.

As far as I know, he did all of the work in his house entirely on his own. He borrowed some tools and machinery from me for that purpose, like winches and scaffolding.

Herr Prikopil called me in mid July this year and said he wanted to borrow my trailer. I told him that there was no problem and that the trailer was in front of the event hall. He came an hour later, accompanied by a young woman. She was standing with Herr Priklopil in front of the door. Both of them waited for me to come out of the hall. As I opened the door, he introduced the young woman as his acquaintance, but never mentioned her name.

We shook hands and she greeted me politely. She made a cheerful, happy impression. I was very surprised, and could not determine whether she was his girlfriend or just a friend. Unfortunately, I had only a little time and had to say goodbye shortly afterwards. I obviously did not know at the time that it was Natascha Kampusch. Only after the police questioning I was shown a picture and I recognised the young woman.

Police later hinted that undercover officers were mingling with journalists in the crowd to try to detect any facial tics or body language that might have suggested he was being economical with the truth. Later they reported that he was in no way suspected of having anything to do with either the kidnap or subsequent imprisonment of Natascha.

The most extraordinary outing of all, and one that Natascha at first denied before her lawyers issued a statement contradicting their client, was to the ski slopes of a top Austrian resort; a place crowded with holiday-makers, laughing, joking, skiing, walking within feet of her. Natascha's grand day out was in February 2006, shortly after she was first allowed out of the house, in the ski resort of Hochkar, 150 kilometres from No. 60 Heinestrasse.

Furthermore, Priklopil was pulled over by police officers at a routine traffic check on the same day. Natascha did nothing. She stayed in her seat. She smiled at the policeman. She remained captive.

When a German magazine revealed that she had been on this ski holiday with Priklopil, Natascha vehemently denied the allegations, while her lawyers threatened their customary legal actions.

Talking to Austria's biggest newspaper, *Kronen Zeitung*, she dismissed the reports about her trip as 'nonsense' and said: 'I never was skiing. Who says that? It is all nonsense.' One of her lawyers, Dr Gerald Ganzger, threatened the press with lawsuits and said that his firm would go hard against any infringements of Natascha's personal rights.

'We already have a thick folder of such infringements,' Dr Ganzger went on to say, speaking of press reports he claimed his firm was about to challenge legally. But at the same time he in a way implicitly prepared the public for the revelations that were to come: 'As Kampusch managed to flee, she weighed a mere 42 kilos, suffered from malnutrition and heart and circulation problems. If I kidnap someone, keep them hostage on a ship and give them caviar, it wouldn't change the fact that they are a prisoner.'

However, within a day of the denials, evidence compelled the law firm to admit that there had indeed been a ski trip. Natascha's other lawyer, Dr Gabriel Lansky, clearly felt damage limitation was in order after Natascha's initial denial of such a trip. He said: 'If one would put oneself in that situation at least for a second, then one would understand that a captive's excursion to the ski slopes is not really appropriate for getting the first chance of escape in their lives. This needs to be clear: Kampusch had only one chance of escape.'

Dr Lansky said that he and his client kept silent about the excursion because of concerns that the revelation could have trivialised the kidnapping, adding: 'We will not allow any attempts to make up new stories and perpetuate the media spiral in order to turn the victim into a perpetrator.'

He went on to say: 'She was a prisoner for eight and a half years. Her sole contact with the outside world was her kidnapper and media like the Ö1 radio station. And there were no programmes with titles like "How to behave as a kidnap victim".'

Natascha's lawyers also speculated that Přiklopil was searching for some 'kick' through such a brazen outing with his reluctant captive, while Natascha herself later said that she *did* try to tell a woman who she was while in a ladies' lavatory in the resort. Unfortunately, the woman was a tourist who spoke no German.

And so Natascha returned, a reluctant hostage but by no means a helpless one. In his home she carried on with her faux-wifely duties, until the real Frau Priklopil in the shape of his doting mother came to stay – and then it was back in the dungeon until she had gone.

There was one compensation, however, in Frau Priklopil's visits: although it meant prolonged time underground, Natascha had to admit that the house was 'spotless' after she had been.

Natascha obviously came to learn a great deal about the bond between mother and son, and she developed strong feelings for her although she never once met her while in captivity. Through the words of her captor and the images that he showed her of the family on numerous holidays and outings, she came to love and respect her.

Waltraud Priklopil was, ultimately, the benchmark by which Wolfgang judged all women. Whether or not he thought that Natascha Kampusch ever came close to this perfect ideal during all the years they shared together is a secret he took to his lonely death with him.

All the sightings, the police stop, the unsuccessful attempts to alert store staff that she wanted to be freed from the bonds of the last eight years, indicate that Natascha kept true to the vow that she made to herself as a twelve-year-old girl: that she would one day be free. Yet the missed opportunities to run were to rebound on her within weeks of freedom, when it finally came, and to raise questions about why she chose to end her imprisonment exactly when she did.

Trying to imagine what was going on in Priklopil's mind during those long years is nearly impossible. Very little is known. But Priklopil, his emotions stunted by his own discordant childhood relations with his father and his extraordinary reliance on his mother, continued to drink in the little truck-stop bar called Christine's throughout the entire period of Natascha's confinement. He would have propped up the bar and listened as her father bemoaned the lack of a police breakthrough, earwigged as regulars spoke of the family heartbreak, and seen the face of Natascha in the 'Missing' poster fade to yellow.

Nothing, however, would dent his conviction that the prize was worth all the pain – other people's pain.

In the search for answers, police attention has become focused on the Commodore 64 computer found in Priklopil's house. For a man with an inordinate amount of knowledge about technology, who subscribed to ten techie magazines and who filled his house with the latest in alarms, buzzers, sensors and other security devices, the computer remains, like its owner, something of a conundrum.

By any standard the computer was obsolete. The beige-coloured machine was popular in the 1980s but is now considered an antique, though some electronic dance acts still use it, and it is beloved by amateurs of retro-computers. Its very age makes it a challenge for police to crack, because its memory does not function like those of modern-day laptops or PCs. Any attempt to download its secrets will result in some data loss: detectives hope that this will not destroy vital clues – if they exist – as to how he came to choose Natascha as a victim and how he prepared for it both mentally and physically. A Commodore 64 had external storage, in the form of floppy disks or tapes, and police are currently taking counsel from electronics experts about the best way forward in a bid to extract its secrets.

And secrets there must be. Experts and police concluded that Priklopil was one of two things: he was a paedophile or he was asexual. The latter has been all but ruled out, leaving investigators to conclude that he was a sexual scavenger of the worst kind.

A theoretical understanding of Priklopil's disorder has been developed through clinical studies of paedophilia. Paedophiles rarely operate alone. The very compulsion that draws them towards the forbidden objects of their desire by its nature also draws them into a clandestine world of fellow predators. Excitement is gained through images of those they abuse, hold captive or otherwise torment. Images and the fantasies they ignite are the high-octane fuel for paedophiles. Lawmen at the heart of the investigation told the authors that it is those images they continue to search for. It is still not known whether Natascha was sexually abused and she has refused to answer questions about 'intimate personal matters', but the profile of Priklopil is relevant and important in the study of such individuals and what they are capable of, so that other children can be saved from such a terrible fate.

Christoph Joseph Ahlers, a prominent German psychologist who is treating paedophiles at the renowned Charité clinic in Berlin, emphasised the unique nature of the case:

> The Kampusch case corresponds to a pattern well known in the study of paedophilia, when a paedophile kidnaps a small girl and spends years living with her.
>
> It is not unusual and happens very often – but only in the paedophile's imagination. To this very day I have not heard of this fantasy ever having been turned into reality by someone. The closest attempts only lasted for a short period of time, and many ended with the death of the victim.
>
> The reason for that is probably that it is very difficult, if not impossible, to realise that fantasy and actually get away with it. In that sense the puzzling Kampusch case is a unique phenomenon throughout the world.

Ten years ago paedophilia was a taboo subject, rarely discussed by the mainstream media. The floodgates were only opened to stories revealing child abuse in homes, schools and congregations across the world, encouraging investigation and prosecution, after the Dutroux case in Belgium; the monster who kept children in his cellar, raping them and offering them to his friends to do the same. Police believe the exposure that the Dutroux case garnered may have fuelled Priklopil's desires and tipped him over the edge from daydreaming into action.

'I was a stroppy little madam,' said Sabine Dardenne, one of Dutroux's victims who lived. So was Natascha Kampusch, by all accounts. Her kindergarten teacher, who watched her TV interview, testified to that. She remarked at one stage how Natascha seemed to have to use all her strength to rein herself in when she didn't like the way a question was put to her. 'That's how I remember her, always impulsive, always having to be right,' she said.

A child's stroppiness, assertiveness, meekness or pliability – nothing excuses the crime of paedophilia. Yet Natascha insists that whatever took place between them was consenting, which of course it could not have been. If sexual abuse occurred it could not, legally, have been by consent prior to the age of 16. Thereafter, if there were any consensual acts, the issue of consent must be morally compromised by the fact this young girl had been held hostage in such unnatural circumstances.

This much is certain: Wolfgang Priklopil thought that what he had done to that little girl over the course of 3,096 days warranted nothing less than his death.

A significant percentage of individuals with this disorder were sexually abused as children. There are those who argue that paedophilia may also result from feelings of inadequacy with same-age peers, and therefore a transfer of sexual urges to children. This disorder is characterised by either intense sexually arousing fantasies, urges, or behaviours involving sexual activity with a prepubescent child (typically aged thirteen or younger). To be considered for this term, the individual must be at least sixteen years old and at least five years older than the child.

It is accepted that paedophilia is not a disease and that it cannot be 'cured'– it is therefore by definition lifelong and compulsive behaviour. Because of this there will always be a risk that the individuals it refers to, and who already have a conviction for a relevant offence, may reoffend.

Paedophiles are usually attracted to children of a particular sex, although some are attracted to both sexes. In the case of attraction to boys it is normally, though not exclusively, to pre-pubertal boys. In the case of girls, the majority are attracted to girls aged eleven to fifteen.

Paedophiles will often engage in sexual activity with a large number of children, case studies have shown. Until now there is nothing to indicate that Priklopil ever had that sort of contact with other children. But the so-called situational abusers are well known to medical and criminal research: people who may feel sexual attraction to a particular child but do not necessarily have a sexual attraction to children in general, or simply focus on one single victim and became obsessed with them.

Judging from the evidence so far, Wolfgang Priklopil fits the bill of situational abuser exactly.

The protagonist of *The Collector* is not the only literary figure with whom Priklopil invites comparison. A notorious literary invention out of the pen of one of the greatest masters of the twentieth-century novel famously portrayed exactly one such 'situational paedophile', and became an artistic benchmark in analysing the disorder of paedophilia. And it comes disturbingly close to the Austrian story that sickened the world.

Could Priklopil have been the Austrian proletarian version of probably the best-known literary paedophile, Professor Humbert Humbert in Vladimir Nabokov's scandalous masterpiece, the 1955 novel *Lolita*?

Meticulous and pedantic, the deviate paedophile Humbert does to a certain extent bear an uncanny resemblance to the invisible man from Strasshof. Humbert lost his childhood sweetheart to a deadly disease and both developed and nourished a lifelong perverted fixation, in contrast to his otherwise fastidious nature, for what he called nymphets; pre-adolescent female children he found sexually alluring.

But Humbert, like Priklopil, becomes obsessed with only one single child, his twelve-year-old stepdaughter Dolores Haze, or Lolita. He only marries Lolita's mother, Charlotte, in order to be close to Lolita, and eventually seduces her after the mother is killed in a car accident.

With her mother out of the way, Humbert ventures into a paedophile relationship with Lolita, posing as her father. Not unlike Priklopil, Humbert becomes deeply paranoid, fearing pursuit and eventual discovery, and he suffers jealous anxieties about losing his precious prey to another man. Rather than locking away the child he abducted from normality, he starts with her a life on the road – a different kind of kidnapping – moving from one place to another in the hope of being able to hide his criminality from society.

Although Humbert is aware somewhere in the back of his mind that his attempt to forge a marriage-like union with his child victim is doomed, he, like his lowly real-life counterpart Priklopil, partially succeeds in becoming Lolita's friend and a father-like figure, as well as her lover. Experts have speculated that in his complex relationship with Natascha, Priklopil played the roles of 'a father, a brother, a friend and most probably a lover'.

His mind clouded and his will consumed by his sickly infatuation, Humbert gradually comes to fulfil Lolita's every wish but eventually does lose her to another paedophile. After embarking on a quest that only ends some years later, he sees Lolita, now aged seventeen, married and pregnant, for the last time. But this time his distorted passion is spent: Humbert now only sees the shadow of the nymphet he once imagined her to be, because as a grown woman she is no longer attractive to him.

Despite the essential difference – Lolita was not kept imprisoned and brutally punished whenever her captor found it necessary – the parallels between the fiction and the real life story are striking. Like Lolita, Natascha had also learned with time how to deal with her captor and even how to assume control in certain situations; for example, when she, in her own words, 'forced' him to celebrate Christmas and give her presents.

Humbert loses his diabolical attachment to Lolita when the child grows into a woman. Top psychiatrists and even Natascha herself have speculated that Priklopil, too, was towards the end simply defeated by the fact that his once helpless victim had developed into a young woman in many ways stronger than himself.

It is possible that he, like Humbert, might have lost some of his attraction to her, realising that his demented fantasies were never to become true.

She grew up. The mirror cracked. The spell was breaking.

'He could not handle the increasingly independent, grown-up woman she'd become, and I am sure that he wanted to get rid of her in some way,' a psychiatrist said, adding that Priklopil probably 'consciously or unconsciously wanted her to escape'.

As Lolita is becoming increasingly detached from her pathological captor Humbert, he tries to intimidate her into believing that the outside world would offer her no better alternative, just as Priklopil tried, and sometimes partially succeeded, to plant his paranoid, insane ideas into Natascha's mind. But at one point Humbert utters what now might seem an eerie prophecy of Natascha's present – another example of life following fiction.

Talking to Lolita, Humbert says: 'In plainer words, if we two are found out, you will be analysed and institutionalised, my pet, c'est tout. You will dwell, my Lolita will dwell [. . .] under the supervision of hideous matrons. This is the situation, this is the choice. Don't you think that under the circumstances Dolores Haze had better stick to her old man?'

High-tech equipment must be deployed in a bid to find out Priklopil's secrets, but experts need nothing electronic to debrief Natascha about her time in captivity, particularly the months between February and August 2006 when she tasted this freedom of a kind. For this they need infinite patience and care.

Listening to her account brought Professor Berger and his team to their limits as psychiatrists. Because what she went through was unique, there were no textbooks to work from when it came to therapy for her.

'We had no previous experience to draw on,' said Professor Berger. 'There wasn't a textbook case for someone like Natascha – she wrote the textbook.'

Academia does not have a record of a criminal with Priklopil's profile, nor of a victim who suffered an ordeal comparable to what Natascha had to endure for almost a decade.

We can learn something from the trauma research of the fifties and the sixties, from the cases of former concentration camp prisoners,' said Berger, adding that the 1945 report of the famous Vienna psychiatrist Dr Viktor E. Frankl about how he survived in Auschwitz, the most notorious death camp of them all, will be valuable in dealing with Natascha's mental scars.

In his book entitled *Man's Search for Meaning*, Dr Frankl gives a chilling account of the death camp existence between 'vegetating' and 'internal victory' and describes in detail how 'an abnormal reaction in an abnormal situation' slowly becomes 'normal behaviour'.

While he was imprisoned in Auschwitz and expected each day to be his last, Dr Frankl developed his own spiritual exercises in which he would speak to himself in his mind for hours and would analyse and re-enact seemingly irrelevant everyday things he had experienced in his life before he was incarcerated there. At the same time, he never erased from his consciousness the constant threat of death that was lurking throughout every single second of his captivity.

The doctors say that this is exactly the path Natascha went down from that first day. She constantly had to fear for her own life when Priklopil locked her up in the concrete cellar behind the 150-kilo steel door that could have easily become her tomb if anything were to have happened to him. But in contrast to the concentration camp survivors, the innocent child was also made to fear for her captor's life, as he constantly repeated that he would kill himself if she tried to break out.

Psychologist Philipp Schwärzler, from the Child Protection Centre in Vienna, likewise compared Natascha's situation to that of the victims of the worst manmade horror of the twentieth, or any other, century – the concentration camp inmate. 'Humans function by their will to survive, which makes its way through in the most terrible situations,' Schwärzler said.

He went on: 'In order to do this, the psyche uses a protection mechanism: stop thinking, detach and discard anything dreadful. No person can live in constant resistance, because that only tortures them further. To live with the unbearable may not be healthy, but in emergency situations, it's necessary for survival.'

And Christoph Stuppäck, chief physician at the University Clinic for Psychiatry in Salzburg, said the Stockholm syndrome is, especially for these reasons, very pronounced in Natascha Kampusch's case. 'To identify with your aggressor is a survival strategy. If you can't conquer the enemy then you show solidarity with him,' he says, indicating why she felt unable to escape on prior occasions even though the slightest of chances may have been there.

'When you only have one person as an attachment figure, you lose the ability to communicate,' says Stuppäck. 'All the experiences that you have on your way to becoming an adult were taken away from her.'

Schwärzler also says that one could rebuild the capability for bonding and relationships. Even with the best of therapies, however, Natascha's martyrdom cannot be undone. 'She will have to learn to live with it. That will take a long, long time.'

But Natascha's supreme psychological strength is evident. When asked if she really was, eventually, the stronger of the two, Dr Berger only said, 'There is a simple answer to that: her survival is the proof of her strength. She is alive, he is dead.'

7

Breakout

Wolfgang Priklopil planned and executed the taking of Natascha Kampusch with the precision of the engineer he was. In contrast, her choice to free herself from his grip on 23 August 2006 was as spontaneous as the decisions of an eighteen-year-old girl should be when choosing a new hairband or picking a new shade of lip gloss. Impulse, not planning, told her that D-Day had arrived.

Several times before, she had gone towards the garden gate at No. 60 Heinestrasse, that alarmed, mute sentinel guarding her captor's domain, fully intent on crossing the boundary into a universe beyond Planet Priklopil, only to be drawn back into his strange orbit. She was pulled by the conflicting forces of fear, apprehension and, probably, a kind of affection for the man who brought her up.

Even love?

She had tried, albeit unsuccessfully, to catch the eyes of strangers in stores, to communicate who she was with pleading looks and a smile which she tried to make as similar to that in her schoolgirl photo as it was possible to do, on numerous occasions. She had cried in frustration, dreamed of her parents, written down her deepest feelings in exercise books she managed to keep secret from him – and now, on this day, at 12.53 p.m. Central European Time, all the gods were smiling on her. Wolfgang Priklopil decided it was a good day to clean his car.

Rather, he thought it was a good day to let his prized possession clean it for him. No stress for him, and a breath of fresh air for her in the big outside. What could be better?

It was time for Natascha Kampusch to grow up and get out.

The weather was good. Natascha was given his vacuum cleaner and told, as always, that he would be 'right beside you'. As if she needed reminding. He was an aura, omnipresent, ready to pounce if his illusion of keeping this perfect woman-child should ever be endangered.

In the end the techno-freak was brought down by that most indispensable of personal technological items of the twenty-first century – the mobile telephone.

He took a call as Natascha did what she was instructed to do – first clean the driver's side of his beloved BMW before moving on to the passenger cockpit and finally the back seat. On the line was a man enquiring about renting the apartment in the Hallergasse that Priklopil had renovated with Natascha's help.

The noise of the vacuum cleaner coupled with the poor reception just where he was standing made Priklopil drop his guard momentarily. He was charming on the phone to the young Austrian IT technician who was asking about the property, when it would be ready and how much he wanted to rent it for.

Unbeknown to the caller, he had released a young woman from captivity. A banal enquiry to a banal man broke the chains that bound her for over eight long years.

Wolfgang K's boss was later called back by police to be told how his employee's innocent enquiry about somewhere to live had ended the nightmare for Natascha, her family and for everyone who cared for them. He in turn told Wolfgang how his simple telephone call had brought the tragedy to closure. Herr K – his full name has not been revealed by police at his request – is still flabbergasted to think of his role in history:

I was looking for a flat to rent. I found this ad on the Internet about the flat in the Hallergasse in Vienna's Rudolfsheim district.

It took quite a while before Herr Priklopil answered the phone. But I actually thought that I was speaking to Herr Holzapfel. I remember that conversation clearly, although I had spoken to many people on that day, because he was one of the very few that were polite to me. And he sounded a very serious man.

He finished the conversation in a very normal way and we agreed to meet on Friday evening. He was not at all nervous or excited in any way. The conversation can't have lasted for more than a few minutes.

I am happy to have helped her, but I am sure that she would have been escaping that tyranny sooner or later. I think she should be left in peace. I hope she can find a normal life. I don't want to be over-estimated, I'm just a small cog in her story.

Far from it. He was a Ferris wheel in the saga, which just happened to stop at the right place at the right time.

Still barely able to explain it when she appeared on TV just fourteen days later in one of the most watched programmes ever screened in Austria, she admitted: 'I just knew that if not then, then maybe never. I looked over at him. He had his back to me. Just moments before then I had told him that I couldn't live any more like that. That I would try to escape. And well, I thought, if not now . . .'

Yet at the same time as she was closing the door on his life, it was nonetheless a shared life, one that had its highlights, tenderness, tears, laughter: the full spectrum of human emotions divided into 74,304 hours that were far from all bad. By her own admission Priklopil had saved her from drugs, from tobacco, from bad people, from wrong decisions. However warped her rationale, there would always be – will always be – a place in her heart and her head for the man she 'sat in the same boat with' on this voyage through life.

Even in the nano-seconds that it took her brain receptors to kick in, to tell her to run like the devil if she was ever going to break free, Natascha's caring side also demanded to be heard:

I was also really worried about ruining the perceptions of his mother, his close friends and his neighbours. And of destroying them. I mean, to them he was a nice, helpful man. Always friendly and always correct. I didn't want to do it to his mum, to show her the other side of her son. He had always told me what a good relationship they had. That she loved him and that he liked her.

I feel really very sorry for Frau Priklopil. That her perceptions of her son have been destroyed. And that she lost all faith on that day. Her belief in her son. And her son himself.

And on this day Herr Priklopil made me . . . well, I was fully conscious of it because I was the one who fled, I knew that I had sentenced him to death because he had always threatened to commit suicide. But on this day he turned me, as well as the man who drove him to the train station and the train driver, into murderers.

But the momentous decision had come and she ran. With the electric thrumming of the vacuum cleaner in the background and with his back turned to her, she took the one chance she had and bolted. Racing through her mind were the previous, failed attempts at freeing herself.

'Once I wanted to jump out of the moving car on to the road, but he held me tight and accelerated so fast I was thrown against the door,' she would later say. This time she would make certain he was not able to get to her.

It took minutes for her to scramble over fences, across neighbours' gardens and to the door of an elderly lady who treated her with bemusement and suspicion. Undernourished and a sickly colour she may have been, but Natascha was determined. She feared that if Priklopil came after her now, the old lady she was pleading with through an open window to call the police would be dead. This is how she recalled her flight:

> For me it was like an eternity, but in reality it was 10 or 12 minutes. I simply ran into the allotment area, I jumped over many fences, in a panic I ran in a circle, to see if there were any people anywhere. First I rang on the doorbell of this house, but for some reason that didn't work, then I saw there was something happening in the kitchen.
>
> I had to be very clear and explicit that this was an emergency. As taken aback as this woman was, she would not have reacted straight away. She kept saying, 'I don't understand, I don't understand.' Again and again she said that. 'I don't understand all this.'
>
> She didn't let me in. For a split second that amazed me. But to let a complete stranger into your apartment – you have to also understand this woman, in that little house with a sick husband.

The old lady, whose full name was withheld from the media by police, later gave a statement saying: 'She was just suddenly standing in front of my kitchen window. Panicking, white in the face and shaking. She asked me if I had any old newspapers from 1998, but I didn't find out who she was until the police came.

I couldn't stop thinking about her all night. She had no childhood and had to become a young woman all on her own.'

As Natascha waited, she feared that Priklopil could come at any moment.

> I couldn't allow myself to even hide behind a bush. I was afraid that the criminal would kill this woman, or me, or both of us.
>
> That's what I said. That he could kill us. The woman was still really worried and didn't want me to step on her tiny piece of lawn. I was in shock. What I really didn't want was for a local police car from the nearby Gänserndorf office to come. I wanted straight away to talk to the person in charge of the 'Natascha Kampusch Case'.
>
> Two policemen came. I said that I had been kidna— well, that I ran away and that I had been kept imprisoned for eight years.

Was there a significance in the fact that she choked off the word kidnapped mid-sentence? 'Kidna—' It is incomplete, like the refusal to say where the white van driver stopped en route after he had chosen her.

Later, the full complexity of the relationship she shared with Priklopil would confuse people who had thought the story was a simple morality tale of good, eventually, winning out over evil.

The police, when they arrived, were indeed of the local variety sort, more used to dealing with stolen cars than stolen children. Natascha's account continued:

> They asked me what my name was and when I was born and where and which address and so on. I told them all

that. Naturally that wasn't all that great. They were a bit perplexed and repeated my name and they shook their heads and thought a bit and said: 'That doesn't mean anything to me, that name.'

Then they repeated the information I gave them into their radios. I then basically insisted that they run with me to their car. I'm not simply walking through this garden to the car, I told them.

Whatever else the years of solitude with Priklopil had done to her, they had imbued Natascha Kampusch with a finely tuned sense of her impending self-worth as a media star. In those first moments of safety and freedom she asked only for a blanket to put over her head. 'As soon as I was in the police car I demanded a blanket so that no one could see my face, so that no one could take a picture of me. I thought maybe an irritated neighbour might take a photograph of me over the garden fence and then later sell the picture,' she said. 'I can, as a matter of principle, always react quickly to situations. I knew that I couldn't allow myself to make any mistakes.'

As she was driven to the local police station, the last minutes of Wolfgang Priklopil's life were ebbing away.

In the car, enunciating in her high German speech learned from years listening to the radio, she told the officers where she had been held and who the captor was. A massive police operation swung into action. They had failed Natascha down the years, causing her through blunder and inefficiency to lose her young life. They would not fail her now, they promised. But they did – at least in her eyes.

Within minutes, hundreds of officers had been mobilised. Traffic in the north-eastern part of the capital was paralysed, with literally dozens of police cars sealing off roads while a helicopter hovered in the region of the Strasshof house. All vital traffic arteries were blocked, as well as every approach to the borders, creating mile-long lines of cars in streets like the Wagramer Strasse and the S2 in the city and on motorways like the A23. Frontier police were issued with the registration numbers of Priklopil's vehicles.

Locked gun cabinets in police stations were opened, automatic weapons with extra ammunition clips distributed. The specially trained police commando units were set loose. Priklopil became more than just a perp on the run, another criminal. He was the walking embodiment of evil, as far as lawmen were concerned, and one who had outsmarted them for the greater part of a decade.

Erich Zwettler of the Vienna police said: 'We covered pretty much the whole of eastern Austria to try to prevent any attempts to escape across the border. We used everything we had, hundreds of officers.' As the news spread that a little girl lost had come back from the dead and began to leak out to the media, details of the search for Priklopil were announced on the radio. It worked. Drivers sitting in traffic jams caused by the police operation began calling in that they had seen the BMW with

Priklopil at the wheel, careering like a madman through the streets of the capital.

A motorised patrol spotted the car near the Bruenner Strasse – an area with high-rise flats not dissimilar to those where Natascha had once lived – and tried to follow it, but they were no match for his 12-cylinder BMW. His attention to detail always kept the car in perfect working order, and he was able to accelerate away at speeds of just over 140mph. Shortly after that he also managed to shake off a second patrol that tried to chase after him near the Erzherzog-Karl-Strasse.

Herr Ordinary knew how to drive, the police would later say, somewhat embarrassed that the special courses that officers took for high-speed pursuits were no match for the kidnapper.

Christine Palfrader, whose truck-stop played such a central role in the drama, saw Priklopil's BMW racing down the street as he came from Strasshof. She later recalled watching as he took a sharp curve at the junction where her bar is located at an unusually high speed.

It was like in the films, he came down at an incredible speed and than took a sharp left turn and stopped for a second just across from my place. I could see his face clearly. There were pearls of sweat on his forehead, but he looked composed and took a split second to decide which way to go.

I think he then heard the police sirens closing in from

the distance and took a quick turn into a side road. Only people from the neighbourhood know this little road. That saved him, because he would have driven right into them at the road block they set up down the main street. They would have got him and he would not have had a chance to kill himself.

He must have been a very good driver to do all that and keep full control over that huge car of his at that speed. It smelled of burning rubber, probably from the tyres; we saw his tyre marks on the street afterwards.

Another eyewitness to the chase was Chris White, 26, a British worker at the United Nations, whose offices are a five-minute tube ride from where Priklopil's car was found. He described the police action:

It was a Wednesday, and as usual on my way home from work I stopped at the Donauplex shopping mall for a bite to eat, a couple of pints and a game of pool with some mates. Suddenly I looked up and saw there were dozens of police all over the place, at least 50. At that moment my Dad called and said he had heard a radio newsflash about this girl who had been kidnapped when I was young and that police were surrounding the shopping mall I was in. I walked out of the bar to hear him better and you could see them all walking through the building obviously looking for someone, moving quickly from bar to bar. You could also see dozens of police cars parked outside and I saw cops heading downstairs to scout the large underground car park.

Despite the dozens of checkpoints and, by now, nearly 1,000 officers deployed to stop him, aided by a citizenry galvanised into action by the drama – tip-offs and sightings were pouring in at the rate of one per second – Priklopil managed to pull into the underground car park of the massive Donaustadt shopping centre. He was back in the area where it all began. Back to where it would all end.

His downfall had started with that one telephone call which allowed Natascha to escape. Now it was Priklopil's turn to try to make his peace with the one person he called a friend. The last image of the kidnapper alive on this earth, just before he called Ernst Holzapfel, was captured on a security camera above the information desk at the shopping centre. The camera looks down on a composed Priklopil as shoppers and children move in the background. He doesn't look evil, only intense.

Minutes later he called his business partner. 'Please help me, come quickly,' he stammered down the phone to Holzapfel.

Later, in the only statement he would give about his relationship with Priklopil, which included his account of the sighting he had of him with Natascha, Ernst Holzapfel spoke about this last phone call with the man he once called a pal: a man he thought he knew everything about.

I had spoken on the phone with Herr Priklopil that morning about the renting of his completed flat in the 15th district. He called me again in the afternoon and said: 'I am in the Donauzentrum by the old post office. Please pick me up. This is an emergency. Please come at once.

He sounded very excited, and I therefore did not ask any questions but drove off to the Donauzentrum. He got in as soon as I arrived, and said that I should drive along Wagramer Street in the direction of the city. He said: 'Please drive, we will talk later.' So we drove through the Wagramer Street, over the Praterstern into Dresdenerstrasse in the 20th district. We found a parking place there. He asked me to turn off my mobile so that we could speak without being interrupted.

He told me that he was drunk and had sped through a police control point. He was very excited and said several times: 'They will take my driving licence away. It will be difficult without a car. I will not be able to visit my mother any more.' I tried to calm him down. I knew that cars and therefore his driving licence were 'sacred' to him. I had known him for a long time and I had no doubt about this explanation. He was very excited, and I had never seen him like that before. As he normally never drank alcohol, I assumed this was a consequence of the drinking.

I tried to calm him down by speaking about work. We had a longer conversation about his flat and the work that still needed to be done; we spoke about the renting possibilities, and we calculated the income. All that did indeed seem to calm him down. I tried to convince him that he needed to give himself up and that he would probably only lose the driving licence for a few months. He promised to do that and got out in Dresdenstrasse. As I knew him as a reliable person, I had no doubt that he would do what he said.

I then drove back to the event hall, did some work and had a meeting with a client. At about 10 p.m. I was approached by the police as I was going to my car. Only during the questioning was I told about the horrible deed. It left me bewildered, and I was not able to imagine it to be true at all. I simply could not believe that Herr Priklopil was capable of doing something like that.

At the police station I also had to identify Herr Priklopil from a photograph made after the suicide. It was horrible for me to identify him.

He should perhaps have said identify what was left of him. On 23 August 2006, at 8.59 p.m., Wolfi made good on the promise that he had made to Natascha – that he would take his own life if she ever left him. Passengers on a commuter train heading towards the city's north station reported feeling a slight 'bump'.

Within sight of the famous giant wheel in Vienna's Prater amusement park, where the psychopathic Harry Lime asked his cynical former friend Rollo Martins how much human life was worth as they gazed down on the 'dots' of humanity beneath them in the cinematic version of *The Third Man*, Wolfgang Priklopil ended his tormented existence beneath the wheels of a train. Between the stations of Praterstern and Traisengasse, Priklopil beheaded himself. His body was badly mutilated but the keys to his beloved BMW, which had been found by police nearly four hours before he killed himself, were retrieved from a trouser pocket, along with other personal possessions.

What he did in the intervening hours between that last telephone call and his death remains a puzzle. No one reported seeing him drinking in pubs, sitting in parks, walking the streets. Like the wraith he so often was in life, he was unnoticed by the great mass of the public as the minutes ticked by to his lonely death.

Everything we would come to know of him would be refracted back, like light through a telescope, by the one person who came closest to ever really knowing him.

For so long he had controlled the whole show. He was the main actor, director and producer of the secret drama of Strasshof. Now the curtain was about to go up on Natascha Kampusch, megastar.

Not since Haider and his Freedom Party gained a share in power in 2000 had Austria witnessed such a media frenzy. When news of her escape, and her captor's death, hit the newswires, Vienna found itself at the centre of a story without parallel. Natascha Kampusch discovered herself as the Princess Diana of the common person: haunted, hunted, wanted by a sensation-seeking world eager to feed on the details of what had occurred during those long years of captivity. But as the onion was peeled back, layer by layer, Frau Kampusch, as she insisted on being called in all interviews, baffled the world with her feelings for her tormentor. The relationship with her family was also called into question, and there were bitter recriminations from both parents that Natascha was somehow being kept from them, manipulated by her aides, like some modern-day Manchurian Candidate, into being distant and aloof.

The girl in the cellar was no more: the battle for her soul, her story, her mind and her affections was just beginning.

The first few hours after her escape were spent with the police in Deutsch-Wagram not far from the house in Heinestrasse. Erich Zwettler from the National Crime Squad told local media that Natascha 'is suffering from serious Stockholm syndrome', and there were myriad reports attributed to police that she had been the victim of sexual abuse.

Inspector Sabine Freudenberger was the first to speak to Natascha and quickly made friends by wrapping her in her jacket and giving her a watch. The policewoman said: 'She admired my jewellery and regretted that she never had anything like it. The kidnapper always told her he didn't have any money for that. So I gave her my watch.'

She added: 'Natascha had a formidable vocabulary. Her kidnapper taught her and gave her books. He also told Natascha that he had chosen her. If he hadn't taken her on that day, he would have grabbed her on another.

She was very chatty. She told me the whole story from beginning to end. She told me she spent her days just listening to the radio.'

The policewoman revealed to the broadcaster ORF, the station Natascha would later use to give her – carefully sanitised – version of her captivity and her relationship with Priklopil, that she thought Natascha had been the victim of serious sexual abuse. But she believes that Natascha does not want to accept that. 'It is not clear to her. She did everything of her own free will,' she added. Muddy waters would soon become murkier still.

In the meantime Natascha's family had been notified of her reappearance. When her father Ludwig heard the news that his daughter was alive and in Vienna he broke down, saying: 'I hope, I hope, I hope so much that I can hardly bear it, I mean, I just can't believe it. If it is true it will be the greatest thing that could possibly be.' At seven o'clock that same evening, with less than two hours of Priklopil's life left to run, in the Kriminaldirektion 1 police station in Vienna's Berggasse, Natascha was re-united with her dad after eight and a half years.

According to police, Koch walked in and there was a long pause as the two stared at each other. Then Natascha, who was wearing just the simple knee-length orange dress and ballet shoes she had on when she escaped, jumped up and threw her arms around her father's neck. Police department head Herwig Haidinger said the pair just held each other while crying uncontrollably. Ludwig Koch said later: 'The only way to imagine it is to picture a movie. It was completely overwhelming. She fell into my arms and told me that she loved me. Then she asked me if I still had her toy car, her favourite. Of course, I told her. I also still have every doll she ever had.

'I never gave up hope,' Koch added. 'But I am so wonderfully relieved. She is 100 per cent my daughter. For me it's as if she never went away.' Her mother Brigitta was away on holiday near Graz when Natascha resurfaced, but hours later was back in Vienna for a brief reunion with her daughter.

Natascha remained out of the sight of the media for two weeks. Details seeped out from family members and police sources before the circus of media advisers and sharp-suited lawyers began trying to lock down the story of Natascha tighter than the Pentagon under nuclear attack. Ludwig described his daughter thus: 'Natascha is emaciated, with a very, very white skin and bruises over her entire body. I cannot bear to think where they came from. She is staying in a hotel, with a policewoman and a psychologist. But they told me that whenever I want to see Natascha it would be possible.'

Austrian police allowed photographers into the room where Natascha was kept. The room, though small, looked quite like an ordinary child's room, a little bit messy with light pink walls and lots of clothes lying around, including what looked like a quite smart black and grey skirt and blouse outfit hanging on the wall. The cupboards looked full with brightly coloured ring binders, papers and books, and there was a red handbag hanging near the bed. The world was spellbound to see this 'dungeon', but it was the first of many instances where Natascha would complain that her privacy was being 'violated' by the media.

Child psychiatrist Dr Max Friedrich – the man who would later refuse to be drawn on the disturbing childhood photos of a naked Natascha – is the head of Vienna's University Clinic for Youth Neuropsychiatry and was put in charge of her mental health. She was to spend her first month of freedom in the care of his team, meeting with damaged souls like potential suicides and anorexia victims as the doctors tried, slowly and gently, to discover what happened to her and what the precise nature of her relationship to Priklopil was.

Doctors said that the marks on her legs were more likely the result of a skin disorder than brutality. The claim was backed up by her mother: 'That comes from malnutrition, as she was given practically only cold stuff like ham sandwiches and no fruit or vegetables.' This is in direct contradiction to Natascha's later claims that she cooked for him using recipes culled from cookery books he purchased.

Frau Sirny added that watching the video of Natascha's tiny prison was very hard for her. 'The chequered clothes that were hanging on the wall, that was the dress that Natascha was wearing when she was snatched. She apparently always wanted to keep it in sight – her only connection to her former life.'

More details about what Natascha focused on in those first days and hours emerged through her stepmother Georgina Koch, who said: 'Her first wish is a mobile phone. We went out and bought one straight away, but we don't know if she'll be able to use it. She is always with psychologists and police officers – even when she has visitors, there is always someone there. They didn't even want to let her have a doll from back then straight away.'

When asked if he was afraid that the kidnapper had been violent to his daughter, Ludwig replied: 'He did enough to her. I only have to look at her to know that.'

But the conflicting emotions she felt about Priklopil surfaced within hours of her being free. She was informed of his death the day after it occurred, and both police and medical sources said that her first reaction was intense anger at the police for 'letting it happen', followed swiftly afterwards by intense sorrow. She cried bitterly. Dr Berger, the child and adolescent psychiatrist at Vienna University who is one of the key players in Natascha's ongoing psychiatric care, said it was 'not surprising', given that a degree of 'togetherness' had formed with the man responsible for her incarceration.

'Of course the experience is a very severe psychological trauma, especially for a young person like Natascha,' said Professor Berger. He added: 'There are two sides of the coin: on one hand the victim experiences suffering and pain because of the violence, but on the other hand, strong emotional bonding is involved as well. Eight years alone with just one man that has now been ripped from her life has certainly left her in shock.'

Shocked, too, were the followers of this strange relationship when it was revealed that Natascha paid her respects to her kidnapper by spending ten minutes alone with his body in the morgue of the Vienna Institute of Forensic Medicine and lit a candle in front of the closed coffin. The young woman was accompanied by her psychiatric adviser Professor Friedrich, in what was reportedly a 'solemn and intimate ceremony of grief lasting several minutes'.

Local media have suggested that the visit to the morgue was probably advised by Professor Friedrich as part of the process of Fraulein Kampusch coming to terms with her eight-year ordeal. Professor Berger said that Natascha insisted on seeing her abductor's coffin, as she was not allowed to attend his burial – in an unmarked grave at an unidentified cemetery.

'She wanted to go to Herr Priklopil's funeral,' said Berger, 'but I told her it was not a good idea and talked her out of it. She then went to the morgue instead and asked to spend ten minutes alone in a room with his coffin.' Neither he nor Professor Friedrich said whether she cried during the farewell, but he did confirm the reports that she was angry with the police for letting him die. He said: 'Fraulein Kampusch blames herself for the death of Herr Priklopil and for the suffering it inflicted on his mother. She still feels guilty, but is also very angry with police, because in her opinion they let him die. She blames the police for not preventing his suicide.'

Wolfgang Priklopil was buried in an anonymous grave during a quiet ceremony without a priest in the presence of his mother and his business partner Ernst Holzapfel's sister Margit Wendelberger. The only other people present at the small and desolate Laxenburg Cemetery, several kilometres south of Vienna, were about 20 civilian-clothed police officers and two undercover journalists and photographers disguised as cemetery workers. The bid to keep the monster's final resting-place a secret had failed.

The ceremony only took a few minutes, with the two women quietly saying the Lord's Prayer. They laid red and pink roses and an evergreen wreath with an inscription reading: 'Last fond farewell from your beloved ones.'

The news that Natascha mourned by his coffin and wanted to go to his funeral was relayed against the very public backdrop of her apparent indifference towards her parents. A spat that her high-profile, high-cost legal/media minders wanted to keep a lid on soon played out in the papers. Again, it went some way towards turning public opinion against Natascha at a later stage.

After Natascha was free she was given a psychologist, as she requested. She also contacted the Weisser Ring organisation, which helps victims of violence. She was familiar with their work from listening to the radio during her time in captivity.

Natascha than asked to be put in touch with Austria's most prominent child and adolescent psychiatrist Professor Max Friedrich, whom she also knew from his numerous radio interviews. Professor Friedrich immediately took on the job and then invited Professor Ernst

Berger and other expert advisers to deal with different aspects of her care.

The enormous media interest in seeing the first pictures and having the first interview then led to people contacting the mother, but it soon became clear that she was not the person to deal with, as she had only met her daughter once since Natascha's escape. Natascha apparently distanced herself from her parents and wished to be taken care of away from them both.

Ludwig Koch then tried to start negotiating on Natascha's behalf, and hired an agent, Rupert Leutgeb. He was sidelined, however, when it was revealed that Natascha had been given her own lawyer, Dr Guenther Harrich. He was invited by the psychiatrists, as he had already worked with them on the case of an Austrian girl who had been kept in a box by her stepmother.

But Dr Harrich's telephone lines were instantly blocked with callers wanting an interview, and as a result a professional PR adviser was hired – the PR and lobbying expert Dietmar Ecker of Ecker & Partners, whose other clients include the Republic of Serbia. Ecker was invited by Professor Berger, as the pair of them were friends and went back a long way.

The original lawyer, Dr Harrich, resigned after about a week, admitting that he had been overburdened by the case. 'I cannot deal with it any more,' he said, 'as it would mean neglecting my other clients. I also cannot deal with this incredible media pressure. I would like to be able to go home without having a dozen reporters and TV crews besieging my apartment.'

Dr Harrich himself recommended Natascha's current legal representatives, Lansky, Ganzger & Partners, who are one of Austria's biggest corporate law firms specialising in media law. Thus began the healing – and marketing – process of Natascha Kampusch. It is unclear which of these processes came first in her mind, but the rush for advisers created bitterness in her family.

Frau Sirny was the first to complain that she'd hardly seen her daughter since she escaped. 'A daughter also needs her mother,' she said, railing against the medical experts who tried to explain the depth of isolation and confusion that Natascha was experiencing. 'Why can't I see my child?' was one headline in an Austrian newspaper. 'Natascha is locked away *again* – that is simply terrible for me,' said Frau Sirny, who said in an interview:

Psychologists and physicians – yes, that is both important and good. But nevertheless, a daughter needs her mother.

Every time the phone rang I was both excited and anxious. I always hoped for news of my daughter but dreaded the thought of it being bad. And every so often the police would ask me to come to the station to identify items of clothing or girls' belongings they had found, whether it was underwear, a school bag or shoes. Each time it was like going to my own execution.

At times I even wished they would find Natascha's body – at least then I could have striven towards some kind of closure and had a grave where I could mourn my beautiful daughter.

But instead I continued as if she would walk through the door at any minute. And now . . . now I can't see her.

Nothing would make me happier than if Natascha came to live with me, but she is not a child any more and that is a decision she will have to make. At the moment I'm not even allowed to see her, which is torturous for me.

She is so pretty, just like in her old photos, but much too thin. It's strange for me because when she vanished she was just a child, but now she is an adult. I always knew she had an iron will. It's unbelievable that she has survived such an ordeal and was strong enough and clever enough to escape. I'm so proud of her.

Ludwig, after his euphoric reunion with Natascha, also complained that he feared he was becoming a stranger in the world of Brand Natascha. Aware of the phenomenal media interest coupled with his daughter's determination to map out her own future, he railed in frustration: 'I lost her once before and I have lost her now. I, her father, must beg to see her. Is that not some kind of insanity? Many psychiatrists have told me that it would be for the best if she was with me. Why not, then? Isn't it crazy that I don't know where she is?'

Whatever Natascha attempted to do, or not do, it came across, to a public scrutinising and dissecting her and her motives like those of no other individual, as a somehow callous disregard for her own flesh and blood. It seemed that she preferred the chase for fame and fortune to the love and affection of a family who thought they had lost her permanently. Perception is everything when you are a media star. That is why her media team had to move quickly to try to preserve the purity of the NK image, as she was referred to by the Porsche-driving, cocktail-sipping PR set.

It became apparent that Natascha was the most sought-after 'property' for the media in the world at that moment. One journalist said that if Osama bin Laden had been found and Natascha Kampusch had spoken on the same day, she would have beaten the terrorist mastermind to the top item on the evening news.

Such massive interest, with interview offers flooding in and fantastical sums of money being promised, made Natascha anxious to explain, at least in part, how she was feeling. She did it by means of a curious 'Letter to the world', released five days after she escaped and reprinted in full below.

Dear journalists, reporters, and people of the world.

I realised quite early what a strong impression the news of my captivity has made on people, but I ask for understanding in satisfying the tremendous interest of the public. I realise how shocking and worrying the thoughts about my time in my prison must be, and that something like this could even be possible. I also realise there is a certain amount of curiosity and a desire to know more about the circumstances in which I lived.

But at the same time I want to make it clear that I don't want to answer any details about intimate personal matters, and am prepared to take steps to ensure this interest does not get out of control.

She then goes on to release some details of her captivity:

My personal space: my room was equipped with everything I would need and I made it my home, and it was not meant to be shown to the public.

My daily life: This was carefully regulated, mostly it started with a joint breakfast – he was anyway not working most of the time. There was housework, reading, television, talking, cooking. That's all there was, year in and year out, and always tied in with the fear of being lonely.

On my relationship: He was not my master. I was just as strong as him, but he would, symbolically speaking, sometimes be my support and sometimes be the person who kicked me. But with me he had picked the wrong person, and we both knew that.

He did the kidnapping alone and prepared everything in advance. After that we furnished the room together, and it was not 1.6 metres high. I also did not cry after I made my escape. It was no reason to cry.

In my eyes, his death was not necessary. It would not be the end of the world if he had simply been given a prison sentence. He has been a big part of my life, and as a result I do feel I am in a sort of mourning for him. It is true that my youth was different to the youth of others, but in principle I don't feel I missed anything. On the contrary, there are certain things I avoided, having nothing to do with smoking or drinking to start off with, and I didn't meet the wrong friends.

Message to the media: The one thing I would appeal for from the press is a stop to the insulting reports, the misinterpretations of reality, the commentaries that claim to know better and the lack of respect for me.

At the moment I feel very well in the place where I'm staying, although perhaps I feel a little bit too much controlled. I am the one who has decided only to have telephone contact with my family. I'm also the one who will decide when I want to have contact with journalists.

On my escape: It happened as I was cleaning the car in the garden and saw that he had walked away during the vacuum cleaning. That was my chance, I dropped the vacuum cleaner and left it running.

I also want to stress that I never called him master, although he demanded it. I think that's what he wanted, to be addressed like that, but he never meant it really.

I have a lawyer who discusses the law with me. The youth lawyer Monica Pintertis has my trust, together with Dr Friedrich and Dr Berger, with whom I feel I can speak. The investigations team were very good to me, and I greet them warmly, although they were a bit too curious, but that is after all their job.

Intimate questions: Everybody wants to ask intimate questions, but these have nothing to do with anybody else. It may be that one day I speak to my therapist about it and maybe not. At the end of the day my private life is mine alone.

To the man who was the friend of her kidnapper she said:

Herr H should not feel guilty, it was Wolfgang's own decision to throw himself in front of a train. I also feel sympathy for the mother of Wolfgang. I can put myself in her position and I feel for her and have understanding. I and we both are thinking of him. I want to thank all the people who've taken part in my fate. But please let me have some peace in the immediate future. I hope that Dr Friedrich will be able to use this letter to make that clear. There are many people caring for me now. Please let me have time until I feel I can talk for myself.

The Herr H referred to in the last paragraph is Ernst Holzapfel, the man she met briefly in captivity and who took the last phone call from Priklopil before his suicide.

Natascha's letter did not damp down the flames of curiosity. Rather it made them burn even more brightly. This clear affection for Priklopil, later to be expressed in print and her famous TV interview, coupled with her conviction that she didn't miss much in life, began slowly to halt the course of the lumbering supertanker of public opinion and would, in a short space of time, turn it 180 degrees against her.

On the night of Wednesday 6 September, two weeks after she had freed herself, and showing her innate love of, and capacity for, control, Natascha Kampusch co-ordinated a triple media strike of TV, newspapers and magazines in an effort to keep a grip on what she saw as her own story, which was to be told in her own way.

Each of the three lucky winners in the behind-the-scenes bidding war for the first interview had signed contracts, all of them scrutinised and the list finalised by Natascha herself in marathon sessions with her lawyers, in which they agreed to pay syndication fees to a foundation of her choice. The interviews with the *Kronen Zeitung* newspaper, the Austrian *News Magazine* and the ORF TV special all came out within two hours of each other, as she specified.

Austria's *News Magazine* hit the streets first. The magazine sold out within hours as readers scrambled to read the details of the girl in the cellar. It gave a clearer portrait of the 'victim' who despised the very term. Speaking to its editor-in-chief, Alfred Wurm, Kampusch said:

> Dr Friedrich is quite OK. He is very intelligent and always knows what I mean. My lawyers and my media adviser are also supporting me the best they can. I have by now accepted them all and they have probably

accepted me. All of them are pretty cool. At least most of the time.

There was a small confrontation between my lawyer Dr Lansky and Professor Friedrich. One wanted me to leave Vienna General Hospital (AKH) and the other wanted me to remain there for a while. Eventually I had to intervene and make sure that this difference of opinion was sorted out.

I knew that in terms of therapy the quarrel was not doing any good. Dr Lansky would like to have me outside, while Dr Friedrich would prefer me inside. At the moment I am inside, and enjoy my friendship with Dr Friedrich.

I have a female therapist but I don't want to reveal her name. She is terrified by media of any kind. With her I can – and this is the whole truth – always lie on the couch. A real cliché: a therapist and a patient on the couch.

When asked how she felt about her new life, she replied:

Well, apart from the fact that I immediately caught a cold and have the sniffles, I'm living pretty normally. I found my way back to normal life very quickly. It's astonishing, how quickly it happened. I now live together with other people – and I don't have difficulties with that.

I have managed to find my way around quickly. That was not difficult, not least because I can identify with much of what I see and experience here. There are

suicidal and anorexic patients here. And I get along well
with all of them, because I can empathise with them.

When asked why she found it easy to empathise with
anorexia patients, she said: 'Because anorexia patients
must force themselves to eat. And I myself only weighed
very little during the time of my captivity.' And of freedom over captivity she declared: 'I love freedom very
much. I am overcome by the thought of freedom. That
should tell you everything.

'What are my future plans? Probably all sorts of things.
Someone with my past will in any case plan for the most
immediate things: I want to be vaccinated for all sorts of
things, first and foremost against the flu. As you can see, I
have completely come down with a cold, and this would
not have happened had I been vaccinated against it. So,
this is only an example for my future.'

Quizzed on a possible future profession, she said: 'I am
still completely open about things. I could imagine doing
a bit of everything from psychology to journalism and
law. I also always wanted to become an actress, because I
have always been interested in art.'

She stated firmly that her relationship with Priklopil
was, for the most part, off limits, once again piquing the
public's interest about what went on at No. 60 Heinestrasse.

'You should not talk to me so much about Herr
Priklopil, because he is not here to defend himself. It
doesn't get us anywhere to go into depth now about such
things. Poor Frau Priklopil surely does not want the

public to read things about her son in the newspaper that are nobody's concern, except perhaps the police's.'

Speaking of her escape, Fraulein Kampusch said it was planned in her mind long ago.

Yes, it was. By the age of twelve, or around that age, I started dreaming about breaking out of my prison when I reached fifteen, or at a stage when I would be strong enough to do it. I was always thinking about the point when that time would come.

But I could not risk anything, least of all an escape attempt. He suffered badly from paranoia and was chronically mistrustful. A failed escape attempt would have meant that I would never be able to leave my dungeon. I had to gradually win his confidence.

It was totally spontaneous. I ran out of the garage door and I got all dizzy. For the first time I felt how weak I really was. But it still worked out. All in all, my escape was successful on that day, considering the soul, the body. And I had no heart problems. I ran out when I saw him on the telephone. I ran into one garden in a panic and started talking to people, but it was in vain, as no one had a mobile telephone on them. They just shrugged their shoulders and carried on their way. So I climbed over the fences of different gardens in a panic, like in an action film.

Imagine it like this: pant, pant, pant and then I saw an open window. Someone was in the kitchen and I spoke to this woman and told her to call the police.

It would have been better if the woman had let me

make the call myself, so I could ask for the right police department. It was not exactly good that the police let me walk in front of a photographer, even with a blanket over my head.

When asked if that was part of her plan, she said: 'No, it was not planned. But I had thought about it. There is a difference between something that one plans, and something that one has a vague idea about, so to speak. It was different to planning. There are computer programmes for simulation. I foresaw the future, but I did not plan it.'

When the interviewer suggested that she must have had a lot of faith in herself, she said: 'Yes, certainly. It was also very frustrating for me to find out that people were looking for me with a digger in the Schotterteich [a gravel-pit pond near Vienna]. They were looking for my corpse. And I was distraught because I had the feeling that even though I was still alive, I was being written off already. It was hopeless. I was convinced that nobody would ever look for me again and that I would never be found.

'At the beginning I still believed that the police or someone else would find me, that someone had seen the perpetrator and connected him to my disappearance. Or that some leads would surface, or that some accomplices would say something.'

When asked whether there were accomplices, she said: 'That is not known for sure yet, but I believe there were none. As far as I know there were no accomplices.'

Moving on to answer a question about how she dealt with her solitude, she said:

I had no loneliness. I had hope and believed in a future. I must say something in that regard about my mother. Many are now criticising her for not being with me. And me for not being with her. But she has visited me. It has nothing to do with heartlessness – we understand each other in this way, too. We don't need to live together to know that we belong together.

I thought about my family during the whole time. For them the situation was even worse than for me. They believed I was dead. But I knew they were alive and fading away because of worries about me. At this time I was happy to be able to use my childhood memories as a way to freedom.

People are doing my mother an injustice now, when they are say bad things about her. I love her and she loves me.

I continuously looked for logistical approaches to a solution. First the escape, and then whatever was to come next. Was I simply to run into the streets of Strasshof, screaming, going to the neighbours? I even had this idea that I would become world famous after the escape, and I thought of what I was supposed to do to avoid having the media at my heels straight away, so that I could have some time to enjoy the moments of my freedom for a while.

Natascha said that Priklopil, by killing himself, 'didn't just make me and Herr H, who drove him to the station, indirectly into murderers, but also the train driver. Because I knew that he would kill himself, I knew of his death in advance. In the seconds of my escape I knew without a shadow of a doubt that he would kill himself. I told the police that, but by the time they found his car he had already thrown himself in front of the train.'

Natascha said she found out 'the next day with the police. The officers wanted to keep that from me.'

When asked if she regretted his death, she replied: 'Of course. I prepared him for my escape for months. And I promised him that he could live all right in gaol because it's really not so bad there. Only now do I know that you would get 10 years maximum for such a crime. Before I was of the opinion that he would get 20.'

Prepared him. The little girl captive 'prepared' her gaoler – the man who stole her from a street – for the fact that she would, one day, leave him. It resonates like the domestic rows of a thousand unhappy, unfulfilled relationships: 'If you don't watch out, one day I'll be off . . .' Did he treat it like a tiff and brush it off, believing that she was his for ever? Or was he secretly glad that the woman-child-monster (in his view) who no longer performed as his fantasy dictated was preparing her way out.

Natascha Kampusch chooses her words carefully: there is ambiguity and total clarity dotted around her statements, depending on what is being discussed. But there is nothing ambivalent or obscure in this statement: She told him the day was coming when she would be free. And he would be dead.

After being told that the justice ministry wants to

change the laws so that Priklopil would have been given 20 years, she said that was good.

'I certainly could not have accepted 10 years. Anyway I prophesised he would get 20 years and I consoled him with the fact that nowadays 60-year-olds are still in really good shape.'

She added that for her, the suicide was 'simply a loss. No one should kill themselves. He could have given me so much more information, and also the police officers. Now they need to reconstruct very complicated circumstances totally without him. But we don't want to talk much more about Herr Priklopil.'

She admitted that she had asked for, and was receiving, up-to-date police reports about the case, and also the grim reading material of Priklopil's post-mortem report.

She was asked about loneliness and said: 'Yes, of course I missed having a social life. I had a need for people, for animals. I was sad because I didn't have either. But I didn't have the feeling of loneliness because I had more time to keep myself busy. I knew how to use my time well, with reading and work. I helped him build his house.

'I was locked up. I never understood why I was locked up without having done anything wrong. Normally they only lock up criminals.'

When asked if she believed in God, she replied: 'Well, that is very ambivalent. Yes, a little bit. I did pray. But later on I stopped. Apart from that the offender prayed. I think even Fidel Castro prays.'

She went on to describe the cats that she missed so

much during her incarceration. 'And I also missed my grandparents. I also felt that I would never see either them or my much-loved cats again. My grandma on my father's side and my grandpa on my mother's side died in the meantime. And also other relatives, my great-aunts.' Then she spoke about her parents:

My relationship with my parents is very good. Yes, I love my parents. Someone got the idea that there is a row going on. There isn't. Apart from that I have so much to do at the moment, which means I really have no time to dedicate to my parents. After all this we will have endless time.

I'm not doing so well right now. My eyes burn, I'm coughing all the time and I find all that to be inappropriate during an interview. I hope that during the TV interview I don't keel over.

You asked before about my future plans. I would like to catch up on my studies. The Matura [A-level equivalent] and maybe a degree. I have no idea in what, though. Something that is quick and easy. Actually everything interests me, and I would have to live for ever to study it all. Right now I'm reading about media law. But I'm also interested in complementary subjects, the – what did he call it? – 'orchid subjects'. [This is a German term for certain arts subjects that are regarded as rare, beautiful, expensive and, most of all, useless for career purposes.]

I have told my mother that we should go on a cruise trip. I don't know where to, but it would make me happy. I have also told her that we should take the train to Berlin once, simply because I think that would be something like teleportation. You get on the train here and then you suddenly come out in Berlin. It really is all about the journey.

In response to a reporter who suggested that the whole of Austria is already 'at her feet' she replied: 'True. But I also want to see London, or New York, but those security measures are getting on my nerves. However, I know that big trips are not possible yet. I would get bad diseases.'

She wants to meet her old friends, plan a project for brutalised women in Mexico, feed the hungry in Africa – 'I know from my own experience what hunger is' – and live in an apartment. If it hadn't been for the appalling backdrop of No. 60 Heinestrasse, she could have been reading from the script of a Miss World beauty contestant.

Professor Berger, in an interview with the authors, spoke of the controlling aspect to Natascha's character, but said it belied a weakness within that she still has to come to terms with. 'On one hand she is immensely strong and very much in control of what is happening around her, but on the other she is quite weak and very vulnerable.' He went on:

Fraulein Kampusch is very mature and has detailed plans about her future, and in the next weeks she will start working on her exams in order to quickly complete her secondary education and then be able to qualify for university. We have spoken to the school authorities, and they said they will make exceptions in her case and are willing to do everything to help her go though the process as quickly as possible.

She is interested in appearing in the media and she is also considering a media-related career. But she is well aware of the things she can and the things she cannot do. For example, she asked for someone to manage her finances.

She will choose a company that will act as her, and possibly her family's, media representative, and then she will probably appear in international media. That is her decision. It is a bit unusual for a kidnapping victim to be keen on appearing in the media after her ordeal, but you have to understand that the media were her only contact with the outside world.

At present she is undergoing therapy with a person who has got double qualifications, both as a psychiatrist and a therapist. She also went to group therapy in the AKH and established a good communication with other group members, some of whom were anorexia patients.

Fraulein Kampusch insists on meeting Herr Priklopil's mother, and they will most probably meet at a later stage, as now it is still too early. Frau Priklopil is at the moment receiving psychological counselling as well.

As for the claims she made for Herr Priklopil's house, all Fraulein Kampusch said was: 'That is my house.' It is a place she knows and is used to; something she could focus on.' [Natascha would later confirm that she does indeed want to claim the Priklopil home under the Austrian system of compensation for victims of crime, to avoid it being turned into some sort of black museum for the curious and ghoulish. She has indicated that she wants to offer it to her kidnapper's mother to live in.]

So far we have not had any evidence that Fraulein Kampusch suffered actual physical violence. She did not speak about beatings and she had no trace of it on her body. There were some blue spots on her legs, but they were not a result of violence.

Control was much in evidence during Natascha's accomplished performance in the ORF broadcast. This appeared to go more to the core of her character during the time it was being pre-recorded (in a special room at the hospital) than it did during the broadcast itself. She stormed out of her seat during the first question, refused to answer any questions about intimacy, stopped during the filming to look at takes of herself to see how she was coming across on screen and, in the words of one studio assistant, 'generally behaved as if she was in Hollywood already.'

As she sat before the cameras, Christoph Feurstein, the interviewer, asked her if she had been lonely during captivity. 'What a ridiculous question,' snapped Natascha, who immediately got up and left the room. She returned after a pause.

Neither was the interview, which was watched by up to 90 per cent of Austrians who own a TV, an exercise in spontaneity of any kind. Rather, before it was recorded, she had spent four hours with her 'media adviser' doing the kind of trial run politicians undergo to ensure they don't get pinned to the wall during debates at election time. She was told how to sit, how to look, how to handle herself.

She was groomed. In much the same way that Wolfi once groomed her, except that this time she had total, not partial control. She crossed out any potential questions about sex, about love, about the true nature of her relationship with the kidna— with the man she spent her childhood with. One scene in which she didn't like the look of her teeth was duly edited out.

'She commands her advisers as if they are her slaves, and they are all very servile,' one person from the elite group allowed access to Natascha told the authors in an interview for the book.

Her youth lawyer, Monica Pintertis, was naturally cautious about her zeal for micromanaging a media campaign. She advised Natascha that she should be easing herself back into life gently. But her caution was met with a blunt refusal to slow down. 'My first instinct was to tell her to leave, to let the sun shine on her stomach for a bit and relax,' says Pintertis. 'But that's not what she wanted. And when Frau Kampusch sets her mind on something, you can't talk her out of it.'

The interviews, the pace at which she dictated them, the fact that she wanted to bury herself in starchy legal contracts instead of smelling the roses as a free agent, speaks, for many, of another agenda and another component in this anything-but-simple saga. The remark from her lawyer earlier in this book, that he didn't want his client to be thought of as anything other than a victim after the skiing excursion was revealed, goes to the heart of this matter.

Natascha's advisers are aware that she must be preserved as a victim if she is to garner the world's sympathy and Hollywood's money. As Germany's *Der Spiegel* magazine succinctly put it: 'Natascha's advisers were quick to discover she doesn't just need protection and therapy. She needs to be managed like a star. And the people who are managing her now are among the best Austria has to offer. The lawyers Gerald Ganzger and Gabriel Lansky have joined the group; they're experts on media legislation and compensation cases.'

Natascha not loving her mother, and staying away from her father, were classified in meetings as 'bad spin'. So was news that she had might have had opportunities to escape before but didn't.

The lawyers thought they had nailed down the bad press with the triple-strike interviews in print and on TV. But public opinion is fickle, and soon the roses, flowers and cards that once choked the hallways of the hospital where she spent her first weeks were replaced by a cyberspace campaign bordering on sheer hatred.

Websites and newspapers were deluged in the second week of September 2006 with hate mail taunting her as being a fraud and a liar, a lot of it triggered when her initial denial of going on a ski outing with Priklopil later had to be corrected by the lawyers. One critic in Austria wrote: 'My opinion is victims act differently than you,

and you enjoyed your time with your "kidnapper".'
Others said 'You're a liar' and 'She is playing us all
for fools.'

'You were a victim as a kid, sure, but no one is quite
sure about the later years,' said another. On the Internet
in Austria it became fashionable to even question her
captivity, with many people writing on forums that her
mother knew of the imprisonment because she herself
carried on a relationship with Priklopil.

That there *was* a relationship of sorts between
Natascha and Priklopil is indisputable. What has
not been confirmed by anyone is whether or not it
was ever physical.

Her father, Ludwig Koch, spoke out about this 'hate
campaign against my daughter'. He said: 'If these
idiots could speak face to face with my daughter
for just one minute they would stop their hateful lies
immediately. She is not as stable after all these years in
captivity as the interviews suggest. As a victim of a
horrendous criminal she deserves all our support, not
least all our respect.'

But the way that Natascha has evaded questions about
the precise nature of her relationship with Priklopil – and
even lied – has turned many against her. This will be the
final chapter in her re-entry into a world she never really
knew as a child. How people will eventually perceive her
will have everything to do with truth and nothing to do
with the threatening embossed letters of a lawyer and a
media adviser riding the coat-tails of a shooting star.

For her father, Ludwig, the media circus is a perplexing one. He cherishes memories of times past, of the days spent in Hungary when life was more innocent. He has heartfelt words for his daughter as she struggles to find out who she is and where she is headed. Those heartfelt words of his are worth infinitely more than the words of those who merely want to tear her down for not behaving in the way they want her to. Ludwig told the authors:

People are always asking if Natascha is closest to me or her mother, but she is independent, she makes her own decisions, as I do. She may not want me to do all the things I do, but I do them and she accepts that. At the start, for example, she had not been happy about me talking to the media, but now she doesn't care, she knows I wouldn't say anything bad about her. And I won't interfere in her private sphere.

My wife had a birthday on Saturday 23 September and she had invited Natascha. It was all planned to give my wife a treat. Natascha and I had arranged that she would tell my wife she was too busy and could not make it, and then she turned up as an early surprise. She was here for three hours or so and she wanted to look at everything. She asked a lot of questions about why we had done what we had done, putting down bricks over the grass in the back garden, for example. And a large part of the house was a small bakery when she was kidnapped, and now that is my living-room. To be honest I'm still not finished with the rebuilding work, and I didn't know she would be coming so soon. I had to rush to try and tidy it up a bit so that it looked as good as possible, and I don't know that I did a very good job in hiding the rubble.

She saw her cat, which she had not seen since she was a kitten. It was a very moving moment. The cat is a grumpy, bad-tempered animal which only my wife can control. It pays no attention to anyone else and only comes when she calls it. The cat won't come anywhere near me. But when Natascha arrived the cat was there in an instant, rubbing itself against her legs. She was also pleased to see we had a dog, our Pekinese who's also called Ludwig.

His wife Georgina said: 'The kitten was the one that Natascha had bottle fed and that she had called Cindy, but when Natascha vanished her grandmother felt it would be good luck to re-name the baby cat after Natascha in the hope that it might be a sort of good luck charm and bring her back home one day. That was why we called it Tashy.'

Ludwig Koch takes up the story:

We were only five or six people here, but I think it was all a bit much for her. She went into the corner of the garden and just sat on her own for a while. She was lost in thought and I realised she wanted to be alone. She wanted to see the room that she had here, but we have rented it out so she could not go there. She also looked at the toy car that I bought her, which I still have, although I had given her other toys away because I wanted other children to have pleasure from them. I only lent them. I told Natascha I knew where they were and could get them back when she returned. She did look at her car and said: 'At least that is something which is alive as well.'

I understand why she was so sad, it was all a bit much. You can imagine, all those years with just one other person for occasional company and then suddenly so many people around. She wanted privacy and we respected that. She needed to come to terms with everything and that was why I asked her nothing. Of course I want to know what happened in that cellar, but I want it to be in her own time. I have not looked at pictures of the cellar, I have never seen it, I have never been there, and I don't want to hear about it. She can tell me when she is ready. I will know at some stage, and in the meantime we just talk about other things. She asked me about her grandmother, she knew that she had died. We didn't talk about it much. She will go to the grave at some stage, but she is not ready yet. She loved her grandmother.

It was great to have her here. For so many years all I had here that really connected me to my daughter was something she had made out of clay when she was in the kindergarten, a little ornament that I always treasured, and then suddenly there she was again – I was over-come.

People are always talking about how she went into the cellar as a little girl and came out as a young woman, but I don't think that means she has changed at all, she is too strong for that. My relationship with her now is as good and as strong as it was then, whatever people say. Yes, it is true that at the start she didn't see her parents much, but she had to learn how to deal with those around her. It was not her choice. It was also too soon for her to do the interviews. They rushed her into it and it all happened too fast. She was suddenly out in the world and had to size up the position and the situation and those around her. Now she has taken stock and taken charge. That is not just my opinion, that is her opinion as well . . . I know that she wants to have children at some stage and have a normal relationship. I haven't discussed with her what sort of job she wants, all I can say for sure is that whatever it is it will not be working in an office.

She has to decide how she wants to live her life. I know that she has a lot of ideas. She wants to start this foundation and she wants to help the hungry, as she was often hungry herself, and help women who are abused and children who are abused, as she was a victim herself. What happened to her is something unique. She said she never wanted to be famous, but because of circumstances beyond her control she now is famous, and she wants to use her graduation from eight years inside – she wants it to have a purpose.

She has a new flat now which is provided by the city of Vienna. I don't know what she gets up to there. She is living alone but has others around her.

She has been shopping a bit as well, buying make-up and clothes, but most of the time that was with her lawyers, although I think her sisters have also gone on occasion. I would like her to have more choice of friends to shop with, but much as I love my daughter, I am not a person to go shopping with. She should be with youngsters of her own age.

But finding people of her own age is a problem. For her there is a huge void where normal teenagers find space for friends, boyfriends, best friends from school, from college, from the disco or the café. Wolfgang Priklopil not only robbed her of her childhood, he robbed her of her social skills too, a deficiency that comes across in her haughty handling of those around her: lawyers, doctors, journalists.

Then there are her, not unjustified, fears that people will only want to get close to her to get a piece of the Natascha action. She is afraid of people befriending her not for who she is but for who she was and who she will yet become. Filtering out the frauds from the genuine article will not be a job for her legal team. She must learn how to do it, just as she learned German grammar in her cell. And the path she is currently on, paved with legal contracts, lined with TV lights, signposted by media gurus, is not one likely to lead to the human relationships which Natascha desperately needs.

But she is free. Some might say free to make all the mistakes she wants to.

8

Aftermath

November 2006. The leaves are falling in Vienna, and the trees are dappled gold and yellow, with various hues of brown and ochre as the days grow shorter. It is the first autumn Natascha Kampusch has seen as a free woman in many years. She is fielding the book offers – between 30 and 40 so far – and the numerous script-writing proposals, TV mini-series deals, movie blockbuster scripts and interview requests that flood into her media/legal team's office every day. She will emerge from her captivity with riches and fame.

She also has her own apartment, but she doesn't live alone.

The ghost of Wolfgang Priklopil lives with her. Those closest to her, and those who have come into contact with her in the days since freedom arrived, say she still thinks of him for much of the time.

'The traces of that are written on this woman's soul,' youth psychotherapist Dr Martina Leibovici-Mühlberger, the in-house psychiatrist for the *Kurier* newspaper, said about her some 50 days after she escaped from Heinestrasse. 'She is someone who desperately looks for guidance and suppresses her growing fears below the conscious surface with great mastery.'

Conny Bischofberger and Susanne Bobek, two journalists on the newspaper who interviewed her, had this take on her:

She is expressing this extreme containment she feels with her body language. In interviews she uses pseudo-eloquence, imperfect and conjunctive grammatical tenses spiced with foreign words. Her hands are constantly clutching, her eyes are closing to the glimpses of the past. Those blue eyes look so sad but also emanate so much coldness. A mixture of desperation, shyness and arrogance that renders the conversation partner helpless.

After 50 days of freedom Natascha Kampusch still lives in the immediate vicinity of the Vienna General Hospital. The care staff of Level 7, the child and adolescence psychiatry, describes her as 'a rather bossy princess who doesn't say "thank you" or "you're welcome".' Sometimes she even seems to reflect the cruelty that was imposed upon her for so long.

Psychologists speak of a 'Puzzle Personality': from eloquent and strong, when the situation demands it, to ill-mannered and insulting – more so towards women than towards men.

From total isolation into the thunderstorm of the global public attention – that cannot end well. Natascha's body is rebelling against it, she is constantly very ill with a high fever.

Respect and plain normality are what Natascha Kampusch now needs the most. But instead of that she is surrounded by an atmosphere of voyeurism and blunt profit-making. Lawyers are visiting her on an almost daily basis to proof complicated contracts. It's all about money, a lot of money. The whole world is fighting for her.

Natascha Kampusch mourns Wolfgang Priklopil. This man was her only human contact during eight important years of her life; the one who brought her up, the master of life and death. The nature of this relationship is what the media want to reveal at any price, and the amounts they offer for it are astronomical.

'Can Natascha become healthy ever again?' Leibovici-Mühlberger asks. 'Yes. But only if she finally learns to cry, if she lets herself be covered and embraced, instead of treating her wounds with money-making and other plans.'

There is no doubt she has suffered, and those scars, both mental and physical, will take a long time to heal. She walks slowly and with some difficulty and lack of co-ordination, much like an old lady, because she is simply not used to walking long distances. High heels are also a problem, but she is said to like them.

Immediately after she escaped her skin was paper-white and her whole appearance fragile, but now she's gained a lot of weight. This is partly due to a good diet, but the medication she is on is also a factor.

Those close to her describe her as very opinionated, wilful, possessed of a very strong personality. They know precisely what she meant when she said that she was stronger than Priklopil.

Another noticeable trait is the fact that she is a great observer; she can spot the smallest details and is always on the alert when speaking to someone. That is a skill she had to acquire during the years with her sick captor, because she was constantly asking herself what was going on in his head and what he would do next, or what was it that he wanted at a particular moment. Trying always to divine the moods of an unbalanced individual to make her own existence with him that much more bearable.

On the streets of Vienna she is, by turns, confident and insecure. She senses people often recognise her and then she feels like a 'strange-coloured dog' rather than an 'exotic bird'. She cannot bear crowds: the long years alone with just Priklopil for company have made gatherings a chore for her that she finds deeply unsettling. At the time of writing she has not ventured out alone: there is always someone with her.

She likes music and movies, but one of her choices caused a few eyebrows to raise. It was *Perfume*, the story of a man born with no smell of his own, but endowed with a super-sensitive olfactory sense. He goes in search of the ultimate perfume, one made from dead women's bodies. Natascha said: 'It's quite a strange idea, making a perfume out of women. But the deeds of the man in this movie are not judged. On the whole they actually all love him. He plays the innocent, and everyone believes him to be an angel.' That last line describes her kidnapper's facade of normality, perfectly.

One of her inner circle told the authors on condition of anonymity:

One must always bear in mind how ambivalent her position is. At times she might look and sound like a mature, adult woman, whereas at other times she appears to be a ten-year-old girl. And I have no doubt that in some aspects of her personality she really is a ten-year-old girl. She did not go through the normal development phases like everyone else. She had no puberty or adolescence and, more importantly, she had no chance of interaction with other people. Except for that monstrous man who kept her imprisoned.

That is why she sometimes has infantile notions about the things around her, about her future development in the media world and so on. Now that she has made enough money to secure her future, it would be best for her to withdraw from the public and to dedicate herself to the healing process and the completing of her education. She will definitely need therapy for years to come.

I just hope her lawyers will not go out of their depth and will manage the whole thing with success. I, however, believe that this branding of Natascha, the packaging of her into a marketable commodity for Hollywood, to sell a glossed-over version of life in the house, is totally the wrong path to take. It is a road that will not lead her anywhere. In my opinion she needs to recuperate and heal, and to stay away from the public eye.

There is a real danger that the opportunities to earn money could cloud the judgement of those around her. The task of her advisers should be to explain to her the consequences and the gravity of the decisions she makes, rather than simply to agree with whatever she says or even to encourage her in certain things.

One must not idealise her too much, however intelligent and exceptional she might be, for she is still a fragile young woman who has endured an ordeal that none of us can even comprehend. Not even the most experienced psychiatrists, including the ones around her, have the instruments to deal with, or to even envisage the full spectrum of consequences from those eight and a half years of her life that were taken away from her.

The concern for Natascha's mental and physical well-being is genuine, and it is shared by her family and by psychiatrists, who fear that she is placing material success above the very necessary step of finding her feet in a world that, until recently, she only knew of through radio and television. She speaks eloquently and plans grandly – slowing, say some of her inner circle, the healing process. Part of that is discussing the precise nature of her relationship with Wolfgang Priklopil with her carers, something she steadfastly refuses to do. She pledges that the secret will remain locked within her.

This question of secrecy, or privacy, depending on your point of view, is absolutely crucial to how the ending of Natascha's extraordinary story unfolds. It affects not only how the ongoing police investigation progresses and how Natascha herself develops, but also how the rest of world comes to understand what has become a huge, intense, public interest story. Peculiar privacy laws in Austria dictate that newspapers and magazines in her homeland are intimidated by her lawyers into not speculating about what took place in No. 60 Heinestrasse or on their outings from it. They forbid people in her homeland from questioning the precise nature of her victimhood.

They also make the police sometimes look comical in their acceptance of a situation that raises serious questions about the efficacy of their investigation. In the first week of October 2006 the German magazine *Stern* published an article that claimed that Priklopil was 'well known' in the sado-masochistic scene in the Austrian capital. One might think this was a pertinent lead in any investigation. A police detective in, say, London or New York, might think that a trail worth following. Did this S&M hobby involve minors? Did it involve pictures? Did it involve others? Did it involve Natascha Kampusch, either willingly or unwillingly?

The quote from the local police in Vienna was priceless: 'This was his private life and has nothing to do with the case.'

How can this be? If Wolfgang Priklopil was involved in some tawdry ring of S&M perverts who got their kicks luring children into their sphere, how can this be so easily dismissed? We know he was a loner – but we also know that he put on many faces to suit different situations. Perhaps he did have a coterie of friends that few knew about. Perhaps they were all like him. And yet this private life has 'nothing to do with the case'? What kind of 'private life' can a child snatcher, control freak and now deceased Wolfgang Priklopil be entitled to anyway? A private afterlife, perhaps?

Despite the seeming reluctance on the part of the police to investigate the *Stern* S&M allegations – allegations the magazine stands by – the investigation is still ongoing, although at a much slower pace. Hardened officers in the case refuse to accept that she wasn't the victim of some kind of sexual molestation. She likes to say that nothing took place that was not of her own free will.

This has outraged some. One family in Germany whose own child was snatched and raped at the age of five told us: 'Perhaps the mothers and fathers of little children who have been abused, parents like us, who now have to work patiently and slowly to rebuild their shattered minds, might like to hear something more condemning of Priklopil and his actions coming from her lips.'

Stern magazine said it stands by its story. It went on: 'There are more and more indications that Priklopil was involved in Vienna's sado-masochistic scene and that he forced Natascha to participate in it. Even outside the house.' According to Stern's information, she was hand-cuffed, beaten and humiliated. Other individuals may been involved. 'Who? She was blindfolded. No one can say when and how often such treatment occurred. Because of her trauma and captivity, Natascha Kampusch does not have an exact perception of time and place.' The story was dismissed by her lawyers as profiteering garbage.

Natascha herself said that the S&M pictures stuff was 'far-fetched' and she could 'definitely rule it out'. Not yes, nor no, but 'rule it out'. Like she could rule out a skiing trip with her captor, before her lawyers were forced to admit its truth?

She also said she believed her mother '100 per cent' when Frau Sirny denied knowing Priklopil. And she refuses to talk about what really went on between her and the kidnapper, saying: 'I don't ask other people what happened to them in the last eight years. Those people can't change anything and can't help me anyway – so maybe they are just asking out of curiosity.'

Early in October 2006, the police sent a preliminary report to the public prosecutor's office; the keys to kidnapper Wolfgang Priklopil's house in Strasshof were handed over to the district court; and police spokesman Gerhard Lang said: 'The searches of the house have ended.'

Traces of DNA were secured, but there are hardly any useful fingerprints. Priklopil was fanatical about order; everything had to be clean. No sooner had Natascha Kampusch placed her hands on the table than he fastidiously wiped everything – surfaces, glasses and dishes. The police are still examining the network of relationships among the kidnapper, his business partner, Natascha's mother Brigitta Sirny, and her former partner, Husek, as we detailed earlier in this work.

Whatever kind of 'normality' Natascha Kampusch hopes to achieve will never be reached if she denies the truth to herself and, in turn, the world. But, for the moment, she seems content to drink in the atmosphere of fame.

There was speculation among her supporters about the international 'Woman of the Year Award' ceremony in the States, in October, which she was said to be in contention for. But she announced that she would not be going: she preferred to stay at home and keep in touch with friends and family. And lawyers. A new media adviser will represent her entire family in the future: father, mother and child.

The two new interviews she gave in October to Austrian papers were seen as attempts at spin-control following the *Stern* allegations. Her top lawyer, Gerald Ganzger, said readers should not look for answers to the conundrums in the Natascha case. He added with finality: 'In any case, Frau Kampusch will not again address the past.' He was right – she didn't.

Back in the driveway of No. 60 Heinestrasse, parked in a neat manner that Priklopil would have approved of, are the vehicles which came to symbolise the two greatest events in his life: the same model white Mercedes van that he used to kidnap Natascha (he sold the original and bought a new one some years ago) and the super-fast red BMW that he drove for his appointment with suicide.

Christa Stefan, the old lady who saw him in the garden and saw Natascha too, kicks herself now for something long ago forgotten, something now remembered – something undone that could have shortened Natascha's time in captivity. 'I remember my old father back then,' she said, referring to 1998, 'looking at [Priklopil's] white van and being bemused by the black foil he put in the windows. "Shall I call the police?" my father said. "Look what he has done to his car. He's a bit strange." But I replied, "Don't be stupid" . . . and now I go to my father's grave and say, "Father, you were right" – but who would have thought that anybody could keep such a thing secret for such a long time?'

Just as the home where Natascha grew up is now a magnet for tourists, so has Strasshof put itself on the must-see map in a way it never wanted. Mayor Herbert Farthofer said: 'I have heard that people are coming here. They go to restaurants and casually ask the waiter if they can tell them where "the house" – Priklopil's – is. Business people speak of a difference, a different sort of tourist. They are not coming by the busload just yet, but who knows? As for the people in this town, we are just glad it had the ending it did. Everybody just says: thank God the girl is alive. If the case had ended differently, perhaps people would react differently.'

One thing the mayor must struggle with is whether the town coat of arms should be changed in the wake of the death of its most infamous citizen. It contains a railway train wheel, symbolising the town's industrial past. Given the manner in which Priklopil died, there is a debate ongoing about whether it is time to abandon it altogether.

What is certain is that there will continue to be revelations in the case that will keep Natascha's story in the public eye for some time to come. Only Natascha can answer all the questions, but is it all getting to be too much for her?

'She needs time to be a child again,' says her father. 'All this responsibility is just too much for her. She told me: "I don't want any of this on my shoulders. I just want to be a young girl." '

That does not gel with Natascha the Controller, the image that comes across from the lawyers and media advisers. And, however much Natascha may say she wants to live the life of a normal teenager, her world now is far from normal – it's shadowed by her horrific experiences and controlled by the media. Unsurprisingly, she has recognised that since she must live with this reality, she might as well get used to it.

'She's looking to do worldwide deals now,' confirms her father. 'She's lost eight years and she wants those eight years to have a purpose. She also wants to use her fame to help other people.' He went on:

She's not happy about the way certain things have happened. It was all too fast to start off with. She had just escaped, and suddenly she was doing this interview. People took advantage of her and they rushed her into it. My theory is they wanted to cash in and make themselves famous.

Natascha was manipulated by these others. I am totally convinced that she was just putting up with them, then she sized them up and told them to get lost. We have these regular family meetings now, where everyone talks about everything together.

We have been trying to decide on Natascha's future plans together. In the end Natascha will make the final decision. She does hope to have a normal life at some stage. She is living alone in her flat, although with help nearby. She says she wants to get married and have children but it's hard to see how that could happen. Even if she met a nice young man, how would he cope with the interest it would create? People would be asking, and she would probably be asking herself, if he was really a nice man or someone who just wanted something from her.

He stops, staring, trying to block images, he says, of what Priklopil might have done to his little girl.

For eight years, I prepared myself to receive some news: either that she had been found or her body had been found. I had mentally rehearsed it. So when the news came that she had been found I just went into autopilot. I was completely composed. I just got in my car and drove to the police station. Recently, while sitting in our garden she so loved as a child, she told me, 'When I am 60 and you are 90 and walking with a stick, I will still be your little girl.'

But the truth is no one can bring me back my little girl. I miss her and I am proud of the woman Natascha has become, but I will never get my little girl back.

Meanwhile, despite the renewed contact with her family and the attempts to claw back some kind of normal life, she remains under psychiatric observation, albeit as an outpatient. The flat that she has been given temporarily by the Viennese city authorities is just a short distance from the hospital where she was treated. Dr Haller hopes there will be a normalisation in the relationship with her parents: 'That is very important because, exaggeratedly speaking, she has been kidnapped a second time. It is difficult for Natascha to respond to a 180-degree swing from total isolation to 1,000 per cent attention.'

The police at one time discussed putting Natascha into some kind of witness protection programme of the sort afforded to supergrasses in organised crime, but dropped the idea when legal experts said it was not appropriate since she was not a criminal. But changing her name at some time in the future remains an option, and would only cost her the equivalent of nine pounds sterling.

Professor Berger acknowledges that the police investigation, in terms of dealing with Natascha, is finite. 'It's clear that the police interrogation is coming to an end. Fraulein Kampusch is a victim not a perpetrator. The police are not used to working with victims.'

Both he and Professor Friedrich warn there could be some delayed effects on Natascha, like the kind of posttraumatic stress syndrome suffered by soldiers long after the shooting has stopped. They warn Natascha she can expect to suffer headaches, nausea, vomiting, sleeping disorders and panic attacks. The care and support team only sees 'the tip of a dramatic iceberg' in Natascha Kampusch's reaction so far.

Natascha continues to be a magnet for those who praise her courage and unbreakable spirit. Fans worldwide have bombarded her with messages, letters, flowers and cuddly stuffed toys. At the height of her fame, in the days immediately following her escape, she was receiving 100 packages, letters and bouquets every 24 hours. To cope with the deluge, personnel at the hospital were reassigned from their normal duties to play postman. It has eased off a little now, but mail continues to arrive. Many of the toys have been donated to orphanages and wards for sick children. There have also been the inevitable marriage proposals, but she isn't taking them seriously.

'Natascha reads every letter and will answer each and every one,' promises the lawyer Ganzger.

One girl with whom she has bonded in a unique way is a Russian teenager called Elena Simakhine. The reason is that, as a young girl, Elena was also kidnapped from the street and held in a purpose-built secret room under a garage. Like Natascha, she was held for years in a tiny cell, although she was held for four years instead of eight, and was older when seized. However, Elena's kidnapper had repeatedly raped and tortured her throughout her ordeal.

When Elena saw the pictures of Natascha's legs under the blanket as she was led to safety by police she did not need any more confirmation that the awful story was true. Lena's own skin turned the same milky white with a slight tinge of green after four years without sunlight.

Elena was just 17 when she and her 14-year-old friend Katya Martynova were drugged by former army officer Viktor Mokhov and locked in a purpose-built garage cellar. Elena gave birth twice in the underground dungeon, with only her young friend to help her, and both babies were taken away by Mokhov and abandoned on doorsteps in the small town of Skopin, from where they were later adopted.

When she finally escaped in May 2004, she was eight months pregnant, this time with a baby that would eventually be stillborn, and the young woman told the world she would never trust a man again. But now she is married to her new love Dima and has earned a place at university where she is studying journalism. She is even thinking of having children with her husband. 'I would like two or three,' she said.

Speaking from Russia, she said: 'My message to Natascha is private, for her only. I hope it will help her with what lies ahead. Back then I never would have thought that I could have a normal life ahead of me. I thought I would never love or even trust a man, so when my family and friends toasted us at our wedding last year it felt like a miracle. But when I had been locked in the cellar, I had given up all hope and stopped dreaming. It was all I could do to survive.

The man who kidnapped Natascha committed suicide when she escaped, while Mokhov, who kidnapped Elena, was caught and sentenced to seventeen years in jail.

Now 24, Elena says she hopes her correspondence with Natascha 'helps her come to terms with the enormity of what happened to her'. Those close to her say it does. While that goes on, the psychiatric team are looking for her to bond with a special female friend. 'It is important, since Natascha's only attachment figure for the past eight years was her tormentor, that she now has a positive feminine attachment figure,' says her former chief psychiatrist Max Friedrich.

Before the Natascha Kampusch case it could be argued that Austria was identified with Mozart, cowbells, *The Sound of Music* and Joerg Haider. Icons that, Haider aside, the tourist authorities were not unhappy with. Now it is Natascha who has become the indelible face of an entire country, the girl who put a nation of eight million on a map in a way it never thought possible.

She is even the subject of newspaper surveys. The *Salzburger Nachrichten* reported that 90 per cent of Austrians were 'very excited' about her first TV interview, while 50 per cent of readers could not fathom why she chose to live neither with her mother nor her father. Over 80 per cent of Austrians are convinced that the kidnapping victim is receiving the best possible medicinal and psychological care, for which 75 per cent said the state should pay. However, 68 per cent believe that Natascha will never be able to lead a 'normal life'.

Interestingly, over half – 62 per cent – don't believe that Wolfgang Priklopil planned and executed the crime alone.

The 'Natascha Bandwagon', as some newspapers have called this phenomenon, has had other repercussions. After she escaped and details of her existence were revealed there was a massive rise across the country, at least for a few days, in the number of parents accompanying their children to school. There was also a huge surge in mobile phone sales for children, their fretting parents wanting to be able to contact them at will. This in turn triggered a second debate about 'cotton wool kids' and how it was important, after all, to allow them independence at an early age for character-building purposes.

There was even a new illness – Natascha Kampusch Syndrome. Medical experts coined the term to explain the anxiety thousands of parents began feeling about their own children after hearing Natascha's shocking tale. It involves spectacular and often violent outbursts, particularly by fathers who see demons everywhere and accuse neighbours and friends of being 'kiddy fiddlers'. The most extreme case involved a father who set his neighbour on fire because he believed he had kidnapped his daughter.

Vienna psychotherapist Kurt Kletzer, interviewed for earlier chapters in this book, said:

'The Natascha case was shocking enough, but that it happened here in Austria on their doorstep has left many people traumatised and extremely worried about their own children. The so-called Kampusch Syndrome is a natural development of that. These parents took it for granted that their children would be safe in broad daylight on their way to school, and now they have questioned that belief, which has manifested itself in some cases in an over-protective attitude to their children.'

In some areas, panicked parents bullied police into organising patrols to stand guard outside schools, and kids' late arrival home led to police stations being flooded with calls from their terrified parents. In the arson case, a 55-year-old man in the Austrian town of Gmunden became convinced that his neighbour had kidnapped his teenage daughter. He tied the 62-year-old up and, when he refused to hand over the girl, doused him in petrol and set him on fire.

Police later found that the 17-year-old had gone on a holiday with a boyfriend from the Dominican Republic, who took her to his homeland, and she had not told her parents. She apparently turned up just an hour after the attack. The injured man was taken to the serious burns unit at Wels hospital before being moved to the nearby Linz hospital. He has 50 per cent burns and, at the time of writing is being kept in an artificial coma, with his condition described as critical.

As well as Natascha well-wishers and hate-mailers, the police also had to deal with a new crime phenomenon: Kampusch con men. Numerous websites were set up by crooks claiming to be the official 'Natascha

Kampusch Fund' or 'Natascha Kampusch Foundation', complete with bank accounts and addresses to which cash should be sent. Several villains were laughing all the way to the bank before detectives shut the cyber crime scam down.

But it is Natascha herself who stands to make more money than she could ever hope to spend if the Hollywood machine strikes a deal with her. Media reports say she has been offered over a million pounds for the first movie deal.

Ned Norchack, an independent film critic, said: 'People have already had their fill of gore and blood in Hollywood horror movies. But they want to see something else in a horror film, a new dimension of fear. Natascha's story has everything and, what's more, it's real, which makes it twice as frightening. It happened to her – it could happen to anyone in the audience.' Rising Hollywood horror director Eli Roth, who has won respect with films such as the recent *Hostel*, is rumoured to be among those in the frame to direct the movie. The legal team are scrutinising all offers.

So life is exciting, rich and new for Natascha. Can it ever, though, be normal? Dirk Depover, father of one of Marc Dutroux's victims, who co-founded the Child Focus charity in Belgium, seeking to protect small children from the likes of this world's Priklopils, says that can only be achieved through anonymity – and that is certainly an alien path for Natascha Kampusch.

As portraits of Natascha go, the one offered up by *Kronen Zeitung*'s Marga Swoboda, encapsulates the strengths and strangeness of this most extraordinary of young women, highlighting her need to control along with her quest for a normality which seems elusive. It was composed as Frau Swoboda interviewed her.

When all of the fuss is over, will she be allowed to just be herself, unrecognised? She wasn't allowed to be tired for a long time. Eight years of bare nerves when she had to stay alert, even in her sleep. One can't just shut off imprisonment. Eight years alone in a cellar, and now alone in the whole world.

Sometimes there is a bit of ordinary daily routine. The lawyer brings files. Frau Kampusch doesn't like chaos. So many changes in a few days, so much life all at once. Her father is coming to visit. She wants to see the cats. Back on the day when she left home without saying goodbye to her mother, she stopped to pet the cats.

Natascha installed an education centre in the few square metres of the cellar. That will keep scientists, particularly pedagogues, busy for many years to come. There is still much to learn from Natascha's self-education.

Stubbornness and a vast determination to set boundaries: these are the characteristics of Natascha Kampush that have fascinated the world since the escape. Only an extraordinary child could manage this without bending or breaking.

It hurts to think that the entire world is under the impression that Natascha Kampush is strong and smart and capable. I hope she can also be a human being who doesn't have to hide her wounds and weaknesses. Finally just able to live.

But matters fiscal and legal are taking precedence over education. She is determined, for instance, to have the house at Heinestrasse, where she grew up, to ensure that 'people won't make a museum out of it where ashtrays and coffee cups are sold'.

She said that she might let Priklopil's mother live there. At the time of writing she hadn't met with her, but hopes to soon.

That Natascha wants to stop the house from falling into the hands of a third party and become a 'Disneyland of Horror' is understandable. Less so is the rumour that she might want to hang on to it even if Frau Priklopil wants nothing to do with it.

The girl in the cellar wants her dungeon back. Perhaps, after all that has happened to her, it is the one place where she feels truly safe.

We hope this book has shown, thanks to the plethora of sources we have drawn on and the experts who have helped us, that the relationship between them was highly complex. That was key to her survival. However, we hope we have also made the case for Natascha to reveal, at least to the relevant experts, the full details of the relationship. She does not deserve to be the target of the sort of nasty hate mail campaign triggered by what is interpreted as her protection of Priklopil's reputation.

The authors would argue that there is no obligation to protect a monster, no matter how much of a human side she got to see, just because speaking out might hurt his elderly mother's feelings. For the medical profession alone, a detailed accounting of the mores and desires of her captor would be a massive bonus. Stored on a computer file, logged with police headquarters across Europe, such data might be effective the next time another child-hunter surfaces to make all our worst nightmares true. In fighting monsters it is necessary to know them.

Natascha grew up in that cellar but, as the medical experts themselves have testified, she remains in many ways the ten-year-old girl who went into it. The urge to control the way the media handle her story, which is becoming an obsession, indicates a fear of the same lack of control that she had on the day she was taken.

It is the hope of the world, and certainly of the authors, that Natascha Kampusch achieves everything she wants to in a life where experience has been replaced with a yawning chasm. The hope of everyone is that Natascha fills that chasm with love and friendship.

There is no disputing her intelligence, her kindliness – she doesn't want to own a pet because she thinks all creatures should have a freedom denied to her during her formative years – her quick-wittedness, capacity to think of others and innate decency. Natascha Kampusch could have emerged from that cellar and that house as something less than human: instead, she came out as something almost superhuman, able to think of the feelings of her captor's mother at the same time as her gaoler's treatment continues to scorch her soul. That the world, its lunatics and leeches aside, was moved in these climactic times of famine, war, terrorism and death to write to her offering succour is testament to the enormous emotional power her ordeal, and her triumph over it, generated.

The Kampusch story is different from other endeavours of escape, of good triumphing over evil, for two reasons. First, there is the enormous length of time she was held by Priklopil, longer than the male adult captives were held by Islamic militants in Beirut during the 1980s – the only contemporary hostage drama that in terms of media coverage is comparable to Natascha's imprisonment. Secondly, she was a little girl who grew up in captivity. This overwhelming sense of innocence lost in that cellar and that house both numbs the world and stimulates it into an act of collective sorrow – that it ever happened – and joy – that it ended as it did.

If at times we have questioned Natascha's version of what happened inside No. 60 Heinestrasse, we have never questioned her courage or fortitude in surviving it. Lesser souls would have been broken, mentally and physically, by what happened to her.

Natascha's enduring legacy to the world will be to make monsters beware of what they wish for. She is testament to the durability of the human spirit – its capacity never to surrender, but to triumph over seemingly insurmountable odds.

She made a pact with herself when she was twelve that

she would free herself. Now she must hold fast to that pledge as true freedom, with its attendant daily anxieties, stresses, chores and worries – amplified for her because of the past – presents this extraordinary woman with her next formidable challenge.

Index

'NK' indicates Natascha Kampusch;
'WP' indicates Wolfgang Priklopil.

Index

Index

Index

271